13.95
F7

A N D O R A P R E S S

ON GENDER
AND WRITING

Michelene Wandor is a playwright, critic and poet. She edited *The Body Politic,* the first collection of British women's movement writings, in 1972. She was Poetry Editor, as well as reviewing books, cinema and the theatre, for *Time Out* magazine from 1971-1982. Her plays have been widely produced on both stage and on radio, and she has also written many radio features. Her book, *Understudies: Theatre and Sexual Politics* was published in 1981 and *Upbeat,* a collection of poems and stories, in 1982.

Cover Illustrator   Angela Stewart-Park, one time drummer, author and playwright for Gay Sweatshop Theatre Company, now works freelance as a graphic designer in Central London.

D0955175

ON GENDER AND WRITING

Edited by Michelene Wandor

P A N D O R A   P R E S S

London, Boston, Melbourne and Henley

First published in 1983
by Pandora Press
(Routledge & Kegan Paul plc)
39 Store Street, London WC1E 7DD,
9 Park Street, Boston, Mass. 02108, USA,
6th Floor, 464 St Kilda Road,
Melbourne, Victoria 3004, Australia, and
Broadway House, Newtown Road,
Henley-on-Thames, Oxon RG9 1EN
Photoset in 10 on 11½ Century Schoolbook by
Kelly Typesetting Ltd, Bradford-on-Avon, Wiltshire
and printed in Great Britain by
Cox & Wyman Ltd, Reading

Library of Congress Cataloging in Publication Data

On gender and writing.

1. Authors, English – 20th century – Biography – Addresses, essays, lectures.
2. Feminism and literature – Addresses, essays, lectures.
3. English literature – 20th century – History and criticism – Addresses,
essays, lectures. 4. Sex role in literature – Addresses, essays, lectures. I.
Wandor, Michelene.
PR119.05 1983   820'.9'352042   83–8197

ISBN 0–86358–021–1

CONTENTS

ACKNOWLEDGMENTS

The editor and publishers are grateful to the following writers and publishers for permission to reproduce previously published material – Wendy Mulford for 'Notes on Writing: A Marxist/Feminist Viewpoint', first published in *Red Letters*, no. 9, 1979; Margaret Drabble for 'A Woman Writer', first published in *Books on Women*, Spring 1973 by the National Book League; Fay Weldon and the following for parts of interviews with her, first published as stated: Angela Neustatter, *Guardian*, 20 September 1976; Val Hennessey, *Evening News*, 12 February 1980; John Heilpern, *Observer Magazine*, 18 February 1979, © *Observer Magazine*, 1979; and Alison Hennegan, for parts of her interview with Fay Weldon in *Gay News*, no. 185.

Chapter 1

MASKS AND OPTIONS

An Introduction

Michelene Wandor

The idea for this book began ticking over in my mind just after I had edited an anthology of plays (*Plays by Women*, vol. 1, Methuen, 1982), in which I asked each author to write an 'Afterword', describing the genesis of her play, saying something about its production process and whether she felt that feminism had influenced her in any way. I was sure that none of the plays would or could have been written ten years ago, before feminism had focussed a new, questioning spotlight on the experiences of women in the theatre. The 'Afterwords' were factually informative, but they also had a freshness, a vivid immediacy which made me feel momentarily rather fortunate and privileged to get some inner glimpse of the writing process itself.

Writers – in all genres – write in private, unseen, away from other people; consequently the mystique that the written piece (article or novel) somehow springs fully formed after the Muse's kiss, dies hard. Interviews with writers, or autobiographical pieces, become ways in which the general reader can eavesdrop on gossip about the great, and even a curious, impersonal form of professional communication between writers, who rarely get together to discuss their work process.

The 'Afterwords' began to whet my appetite for more pieces of writing which would discuss the writing process, but in a context which brought together the individual writer's concerns, with some kind of recognition of the impact which feminism had had on her/his thinking and writing – choices of subject matter, choices of form and language, awareness of audience. Although it is feminism which has directly explored what kind of relationship women have to cultural

1

production – where, why and how have women figured as writers, how have they been critically perceived – the underlying question is one that applies to both men and women writers. The broader question is about whether and how the gender of a writer has any impact on her/his choices of subject, approach, etc. Feminism argues that there is an undoubted relationship, but the exact nature of that relationship remains to be explored and developed in a wide range of studies; literary-critical, literary-historical – and before I start sounding like a female Polonius in search of Denmark – in a book such as this, where writers themselves try to describe, analyse and come to terms with what the idea of 'gender' means to them in their own minds: their ideas, their imaginations, the actual pieces of writing they produce.

Like any editor I was fabulously ambitious: I wanted writers from every genre imaginable; from all age groups, and (possibly) from both sexes. In the event I knew that women would have far more interesting things to say than men about the impact of feminism on them as writers, and about how they try and think about the question of gender. But since part of the whole point of titling this book 'on gender and writing', and not 'on women and writing', was to demonstrate that feminism askes questions which affect writing across the board, some (a minority) of the pieces are by men.

Having chosen a group of writers, asked, cajoled, coaxed, challenged, occasionally nagged, I once again felt rewarded by the results. Asking writers to write about their writing is a difficult thing to do; no one wants to appear as though they know it all. Often a writer might be the last person in the world who is able to clarify his/her work. Since I was asking people to write about their perceptions of the personal and the political in terms of their own actual writing, there were very few obvious models to draw on. I didn't want totally confessional pieces, I didn't want totally theoretical pieces, I didn't want simply polemical pieces. I wanted pieces which would draw from all those discourses, plus would allow each individual writer to throw in whatever s/he felt was relevant— as long as it had some bearing on writing itself. In my initial letter to the contributors I asked each a set of questions which interested me about her/his work and ideas – and then left it to them to decide which questions they found useful as springboards. That's why some of the pieces take an interview form.

I secretly hoped that when it came to the introduction I could get away with a brief, stylistically perfect offering: here is a fascinating subject, here are some fascinating people. Read on. But one of the contributors delivered her piece with the pointed comment that she was looking forward to reading my own contribution. How did I explain, feel, about the relationship between gender and my own writing? It would have been a bit cowardly to ask others to do what I was not prepared to do myself – and of course it is true that I would never have thought of the idea for this book if the questions which come up in it had not been central to my own writing over the past decade or so. So here goes.

I didn't spend my childhood dreaming of being a Great Writer. I was ill a lot as a child, and read voraciously – Dickens, comics, American war novels, anything I could get my hands on – and it wasn't till I started going to school regularly as a teenager that I realised consciously that it was *people* who wrote books. If I read a book I liked, it didn't occur to me to look for a book by the same writer. The first time it did occur to me was when my new English teacher (Leavis-educated and full of wonderful enthusiasm for literature and the theatre) asked me who I liked reading. I simply dredged up the last name I remembered seeing on the spine of a book. It was Daphne du Maurier – and of course, having realised that this name was responsible for my pleasure, I went off and looked for more.

I have got an old, lined exercise book with some flower poems in it; sentimental rhyming things, which I wrote when I was about eight. I had trouble with rhyme even then (an intuitive child-modernist, you might say), and the end of each poem is an invariable embarrassment as I reached for the right sound rather than thinking about what I wanted to say. I didn't pursue poetry again, until about twenty years later.

After discovering about authors, the next critical lift was the discovery of acting. School (and later university) plays felt like nothing else. Looking back now, I think they also provided a solution to, and an escape from, the turmoils of growing up adult and female in the late 1950s–early 1960s. Acting in a play supplied all those elements I couldn't get together in real life: a world where relationships were fixed (the text of the play) where I didn't have to worry about wearing the right clothes and makeup, except as a character, and then other people helped; where above all I knew exactly what I was going to say, to whom, and what would happen between us. In rehearsals I was as indispensable as anyone else; onstage when I spoke, people listened – lots of people, total strangers listened to ME. Wonderful. Offstage, in real life, things were as bewildering as ever, but there were regular fixes of the secure oasis of the rehearsal room and then the stage. Of course I wanted to be Sarah Bernhardt, but that little ambition got over-shadowed when I left university, got married and had children.

I skate over the next few years; I went on going to the theatre, began to copy-edit and read play manuscripts for a drama publisher, but that was as close as I got. Then a number of things happened in helter-skelter succession. First, from 1968 onwards fringe theatre suddenly took off in all its variety – from agitprop political to multi-media hippie happenings. And vice versa. Also, my marriage broke up, and I was faced with having to earn my living and partially support my two children for the first time. And third, the Women's Liberation Movement started in this country in 1969–70. I joined a Women's Liberation group which happened to be meeting literally down the road – the relative good fortune of living in the right bit of north London – and went to the very first Women's Liberation Conference at Ruskin College, in the spring of 1970. I had never been to a political meeting of any kind before, and it was extraordinary and exhilarating. That sense of 'belonging', which I had previously only ever felt onstage, came back into my life. This was something which was mine, and I had a right to be there.

In various ways I started to write with a 'seriousness' which was quite new: I began writing journalism, in the form of theatre and book reviews and news articles for *Time Out*, a radical guide to London's culture, which had started in 1968.

In 1971 I started the magazine's Poetry Column, which I edited and wrote until the end of 1982. The new radical cultural journalism was very exciting – and in a sense completely free. You could write in a way that proselytised and celebrated, and you had the excitement of trying to define and evaluate new cultural events as they appeared. The non-fiction journalism (I also wrote regularly for *Spare Rib*, the monthly feminist magazine, from its start in 1972) satisfied my newly political urgency.

At the same time I was writing masses of poetry; dense, jagged, 'modernist' – though at the time I was unaware of that label. Later I preferred it to the more damning 'difficult', a term which dogs any unconventional 'experimental' work in the arts. I also began writing plays – the first time I had tried to write plays. I thought of trying to act again, but dismissed the idea, with two small children to look after. Writing was a way of making direct contact with the theatre again.

So beginning to write seriously coincided more or less exactly with my discovery of a political involvement which meant something to me. Creative and critical writing developed as my efforts to understand and be part of, feminism and socialism developed.

Indeed, in some ways, this very parallelism created problems. The prevailing politics – art ethos of the early 1970s was instrumental, issue-based, agitprop, exciting and puritanical at the same time. There was the idea that art was only valuable when it was in the service of politics, when it went out to find a mass audience, raised their political consciousness, roused them to political action. In the early 1970s this was as true of the feminist as the socialist agitprop theatre. I felt waves of unspoken 'bourgeois individualist' as I wrote my plays at home, and then took the texts to be rehearsed in a number of the new lunchtime pub theatres in central London. I was not prepared to go and squat in Islington (as all the right-on people seemed to be doing), abandon my kids, or take them with me in plays touring round the country. I wrote a play about the Miss World contest, which was performed in a pub theatre in 1972. None of my politico-feminist friends came to see it. I was miffed. They were all too busy raving over the latest street theatre. My poetry was much closer in form (though not in content) to that of some of the men poets I knew at the end of the 1960s. A difficult paradox: in life I was placing all my bets on feminism, and yet in art I was being rejected by people I took to be my comrades. I remember one political meeting where a woman denounced all poetry as moribund. I went home mortified by this revisionist need to write poetry, which simply wouldn't go away.

To try and make sense of this need for art, I went back to university to do an MA in the Sociology of Literature. Almost needless to say, the course told me nothing at all about why I persisted in wanting to write poetry and plays. Indeed, I found that while I was concentrating on ideas and non-fiction, I couldn't write the other stuff. To satisfy my lust, I designed and embroidered a large, brightly-coloured tapestry, during the 2½ years the MA took.

After the MA, I returned to fiction. I was still imbued with the idea that mass accessibility was the only thing that justified art produced by people who also saw themselves as political activists. I tried writing a few social-realist plays. They were OK, were put on at some more fringe theatres, but secretly I thought they were rather dull. Poetry was still taking something of a back seat, simply because I didn't know what to do with it once I had written it. In the late 1960s–early 1970s I had read my poetry at the very many poetry-reading venues there were, but had stopped by choice, since I felt uncomfortable at being (mostly) the only woman poet – the other women around the poets were wives or groupies, and I always felt a bit odd in relation to both camps.

In about 1976 I got involved in a feminist short-story group which produced a collection of short stories; the group was important because it enabled me to try prose fiction for the first time, and also to argue out, explore, what kind of relationship feminism and fiction might/could have. Personally it was a useful turning point for me, because it enabled me to stop feeling uncomfortable about not wanting to produce didactic art. Because we were all self-styled feminists, all politically active in some way, but also all committed to being professional writers, we made explicit in our group, and later in our book (*Tales I Tell my Mother*,

Journeyman, 1978), a context amongst feminists for new fictional writing. Looking back, I think that group enabled me to articulate to myself that gender-self-consciousness – i.e., being a woman, and being rivetingly interested in writing about women – was central to all the various things that impelled me to write – fiction, as well as non-fiction. Given that that was so, what I wrote would, in some way or another, be shaped by my feminist and socialist views. This doesn't mean that I write merely polemically. Like any writer, I have a more or less clear idea about what it is that bugs me vis-à-vis a given subject. But fiction and non-fiction are never interchangeable. Anyone who chooses fiction (and one might take the same subject and write a piece of fiction and a piece of non-fiction about it, and though both may evidently be from the same writer, they will have different impacts on their readers/audiences) does so because they are interested in the ambiguities, the indirections, the sub-conscious elements in language and imagery, because they want to work on the rational and the imaginative in the mind of the audience. That's true even of the simplest piece of agitprop theatre (not something I have ever been interested in writing), which tries to engage emotionally as well as intellectually with its audience.

Part of the consequence of the above realisations – briefly as they are described – has been a return to writing poetry which is open form again, which plays with language; and to plays which play with structure. In the context of literary traditions which have always been suspicious of the 'avant garde', this is very difficult, and I have not found it particularly easy. But I slog on – partly because I don't have the skills to do anything else, partly because, purely selfishly, that sense of 'belonging' which I used to find in acting and which I found in the heady euphoria of the early 1970s feminism, reappears sometimes through writing.

A sense of gender has been central to my continuing to write. It isn't that I only write about women, but that I know that that has been a formative centre in my approach; I have what I consider to be a healthy reservation about whether I could ever write about men with as much knowledge and instinct as I write about women. I don't mind admitting that, and acknowledging that at the moment that might be a limitation – but there are other areas of experience which I would not yet feel confident about exploring, and there is so much potential for women writers at the moment, that I see it as an expansion in horizons and options, not a contraction.

Of course I was acutely aware of gender-bias in art, and in my own relationship to it, before 1969. But then it acted as a rather negative impetus; I had no idea that I might ever have something I wanted to say or write about. I felt constrained to try and be feminine – something I was never very good at, and am now relieved I was never very good at. Femininity seemed defined by the amount of time I had to spend worrying about what I wore and how I looked – finding the right makeup, then putting it on properly, and then keeping it on properly. Frankly, I would always have preferred to go off and read a book, but the world would then never have seen me.

After 1969, gender operated as a positive bias. With feminism I stopped wearing skirts for years, and also stopped wearing and worrying about makeup. The latter has been the most amazing relief to me; I've got rid of the mask which was never right, which was always smudging, which never compensated for all the other things that were wrong. But skirts – well, I have started wearing skirts again, and have found a new freedom in them.

I have also started reading my poetry again; feminist poetry has brought out a new audience, and a growing and shared set of reference points between women, as well as a new school of poetry which enables men to see new possibilities for imagery.

The most important thing about this book is that it is written by practitioners. In the literary world there is often competition between the 'creative' and the 'critical', for obvious reasons. It is in a way ironic, because both sets of people are actually writers, and very often influenced by the same things; their approach and function are what make them different. Each writer in this book describes her/his writing – often the same person writes fiction some of the time, non-fiction some of the time. Being a writer defines a particular profession, and not necessarily a particular speciality. I was never interested in including articles which would attack the idea of whether gender and the writing process had anything in common. I wasn't interested in anyone who held an 'androgyny' view of the writing process, or in anyone who had anti-feminist views. The people I asked were all people who had something positive to say about how they saw gender and the writing process coming together in their work. Inevitably, for many of the women, motherhood is one gender-determined element, but motherhood means different things to different writers. The unusual element in this book to some people will be the inclusion of male writers; but it has been essential and, I think, illuminating, since so few men writers are able to understand feminism and sexual politics in terms of a new understanding of themselves *as men*.

Obviously no single book can (or should) contain the final word on such a complex matter; I hope this collection will provide an informal symposium of views, which will enlighten both the general reader and the cultural specialist – a provocative collection of essays on gender and writing for anyone who likes reading.

Chapter 2

AN EXCERPT FROM MY UNPUBLISHED WRITING

Nora Bartlett

Joke: I didn't set out to become an unpublished writer, it just happened. If someone had said to me seven years ago, when I was working on my first novel, 'You know, in seven years this manuscript will still be in your bottom drawer, along with several others', I'd have been astonished. But I think, all things considered, that I'd have gone on writing it. I'm not high-minded: I'd like to be rich and famous. And I'm not indomitable. A friend of mine once told me, 'Rejections should make you arrogant.' But they don't make me arrogant – they make me whimper to myself at night and wonder what I've done to deserve such punishment. On the other hand, they don't stop me writing. I do keep writing.

I started writing when I was a little girl, largely to animate the beautiful Common Christian Given Names I found at the back of the dictionary. I spent years of my life filling notebooks with the invented activities of Letitia, Miles, Justine, Anne with an 'e' and Stephen with a 'ph'. But when I was about fourteen, life began to dislodge art as a focus for my energies, and this stage lasted for a long time. I still considered myself as 'going to be' a writer, and I wrote scraps of dialogue and description, and I kept buying those notebooks. I carried a plot around in my head, but I was much more engaged in living it than writing it. Then, when I was twenty-four, I found myself in possession of the isolation, the immobility, and the blank evenings that come with having a child on your own. I didn't become a writer then – indeed, I'm not sure I've ever really become a writer – what I became was a mother, and what I started to do was to write.

In one way the connection between motherhood and writing was a simple one: for years I'd been running in several directions at once, and suddenly I had to keep still, so I sat down and started writing. But although my life now contained these great empty, silent patches, my days were also, like anyone's where children are involved, a pattern of continual interruptions. I used to think of my novel as being constructed in bits, like a patchwork quilt. But if it was the material situation of having a child to look after that made me write, it was also the interior one: nothing in my life has ever surprised me so much as what happens to women when they have children. At the time I found it awful, or mostly awful, but now it seems to me as if my previous life had been a dim, flat, verbal thing, a spoken monologue that ran on and on in my head detailing the elements of existence as they presented themselves to me. My son interrupted that, and the way that interruption feels, still, is that he gave me the world.

I suppose less grandiosely he made me enormously curious, first about mothers and children (did other women feel as I did, that having children altered the whole texture of reality, changed the shape of the world, made their thoughts and feelings about all sorts of things different from what they had been? What did other women feel, and what were they thinking about?) and then about a lot of other things, because what he kept on teaching me was that he was a different person from me, separate, with a different body and mind and imagination. Not just that his sex was different but that he was quite other, and this made me begin to wonder, as I never had before, what other people's experience of the world was like.

A friend told me a story about her past, and it held my attention; partly because the situation – a woman isolated with a child – was like mine, and partly because the action, or transformation, or resolution, of the story – becoming involved in the 1972 Miner's Strike, leaving her husband, becoming immersed in life and activity – fulfilled many wishes of mine at a time when I felt very far from life and even farther from political action. I kept thinking about her story, and gradually I started reinventing it. It merged with my own life, but diverged from it too, and as I started not only thinking but writing it changed more – I was making something up, things came into the story that hadn't been there at all to begin with.

I was writing, in the sense that what I was saving up time for, and waiting to do, and wishing people would go away so that I could get on with, was writing. At first I was writing a story, but gradually I knew that I was writing a novel, and not always, by any means, but sometimes, I felt ecstatic about doing it: writing, organising, seeing how it would go and what my characters could do together and what shape it would take. I remember how good it felt to be seized for the first time with the form of a conversation, or with a sudden sharp sense of what someone had to say or do, while I was out in the street, and writing it down on the back of a shopping list or on my hand. And also the beginning of the utterly new and difficult pleasure of starting to write on a day when I didn't feel like it, because I had the time and had to use it, and sitting at the typewriter feeling recalcitrant but making myself get my characters in and out of rooms, down the stairs, following them down the street and asking myself, Is that right? would it take that long? Is that what he feels and is that really what she thinks when she sees him? Sometimes the fruits of such efforts had to be discarded; they were just makework, compositions on set subjects. But sometimes on those dull days I wrote carefully and well, I pushed myself to think and write and succeeded.

And all this time, I think it's true to say, I never really thought about being published. Not, as I say, because I'm too high-minded to think about coarse things like publishers and contracts, but because – and this came back to me very vividly when I was asked to write this piece – it never crossed my mind that, if I could only finish it, it would not be eagerly received by a reading world. It simply didn't occur to me that there would be any difficulty about anything but the writing.

This weird innocence was probably produced in part by my isolation: when I look back at myself in that time, I seem to be under a sort of glass dome, sometimes taking care of my child, sometimes writing. And I didn't raise big questions about the ultimate goal of my evenings of writing, any more than of my days of changing nappies. But another factor was also that I had spent most of my life as a student, and I think my model of the relationship between writer and reader came from that between student and teacher, in which of course what you write gets read, and in which there are rewards for effort alone.

When, eventually, my novel was finished and sent off to publishers and rejected, I felt more shocked than anything else. And when more rejections piled up, and the other fiction I wrote kept being rejected, there was an element of confusion in my disappointment. I felt something like – Don't they know how hard I've *worked*? I think I felt each time that a mistake had been made somewhere that would soon be rectified; because *I'd* never been on the list of people who failed. Other people's success at getting their work published seemed somehow unfair to me, as well as enviable: I'd always been teacher's pet, what had happened? It wasn't really very long ago that enlightenment fell upon me in the form of the recognition that agents and publishers don't *care* how hard I've worked.

My 'innocence' – my notions about the world that were too vague even to be called illusions – left me very open to shocks, and the shocks when they came were painful. I wrote three novels in five years, and all of them were much admired by loyal friends, but none of them attracted any response from publishers except those one-page letters, some friendly, some not; one or two containing phrases that still make me wake in the night and writhe. But I think it was good for me to have that blinkered time of starting to write and just writing and not worrying about the end, because it meant that I learned how to concentrate on writing itself, and if anything sustains me (I'm not always sure I'm being sustained) that is it. Writing, not as self-expression, but as a means of telling a story. The story my friend told me reminded me of things that I'd thought or experienced, but was also something new I hadn't thought of, and it pressed on me until I started to write it and continued until I was done. For a year after I finished the first novel no other stories occurred to me; then one did, and it seemed to keep telling itself to me, its situations preoccupied me and twined around events and situations in my life and suggested parallels and connections.

Since then, since the period in which I wrote the first draft of my second novel, I don't seem to stop writing at all. Stories (usually in the form of a predicament or a situation, but sometimes the beginning might be in an emotion or a scene, maybe just seeing people together in a certain way or overhearing something) keep presenting themselves to me, very demandingly, and I think that I write as an outlet for them more than for myself. My writing is in a way auto-biographical – all of the stories I've written up to now are told from the viewpoint of an American woman whose age seems to be increasing at about the same rate as mine – but my writing feels more and more as if it comes out of a pressure to tell stories which are not particularly close to my own life, even though I haven't yet managed to shift to another point of view, to imagine another teller. I write to tell these stories, but I always thought – I still think, except in very wretched moments – that they'll one day have a larger audience. There is no sense at all in which I write 'for myself'. I don't feel as if my stories exist until someone else has read them. And so, of course, since so few people have read them, the sense in which they exist for me is a shady and troublesome one.

For a long time I took my rejections personally: felt that one of the many things that were wrong with me had some-how leaked into the novel and made it unacceptable. Some bad magic, some misfortune, but nothing about the writing. Then about three years ago, in the middle of writing a very long and very emotional third novel, I started to feel mocked by my unpublished status, and that is awful. A sort of lethargy came over me, inspired by the jeering thought that nobody cared whether I finished it anyway. This did deep harm because it cut off my connection with the story, inter-posing a sort of interior editor who read back sentences to me as I wrote them, saying in effect, Who would want to read that? It cut the confidence I had in my ability to write, eroded the mutual confidence between my story and me – wouldn't let me alone as I needed to be left alone to write. I had made for myself a sort of comic public persona about being an unpublished writer, and this enabled me to answer questions at parties about what I did; but suddenly it seemed to twist and turn itself against me, saying that something about my life and my work was not only comic but pathetic, and not just pathetic but contemptible.

I think comic personae have a way of rebounding against the proprietor, but why this one did so, in just this way, is a bit of a mystery to me. I think I had personal doubts about the story I was writing, felt that it was in some way false or bad, but also that it was very closely connected to me. It had very detailed sexual scenes, and I think I was probably ashamed of them – though perhaps more of some suspected dishonesty than of the explicitness. When that novel was rejected I was overwhelmed with personal misery: I had a terrific desire to hide, and I lay in bed for a day, mourning confusedly. Then I got up again, and I suppose something was exorcised in the process. I'm still sometimes troubled by mocking inner voices, still shattered by those short letters I get from publishers. But I try to write as though they didn't exist. I know when I write a story that (probably) only my husband and two or three friends are going to read it, but I try not to think of that fact as the most incisive sort of literary criticism.

Having another child, after a gap of six years, has also increased my stoicism. What I remembered about having a baby was how it gave me time and patience and curiosity; I had forgotten how it also robbed me of time, made me impatient, made me bored. One of the reasons I've been able to suppress my shame and misery about publication is probably that, since the birth of my daughter last year, I'm always fighting the first battle and overcoming the obstacles to writing itself that are presented by family life. I think the children probably push my nose back toward writing as a goal in itself, because just finding time and space and breath with which to write is so good.

I suppose I'm saying I write because I like writing. There's not much difference made to that by being unpublished – except for the debilitations caused by shame and self-doubt. But I think that publishing more would make a difference, not in confidence gained personally but in writing confidence. I feel sometimes that I whisper, in my writing, and I'd like to yell more. I think that if I had tested my voice in a larger auditorium, so to speak, I would know more about its effects and be able to vary them more, play around with them more. I'm not just saying that I'd like more people to be able to hear me – though, of course, I'd like that too.

This all sounds rather sad when it's written down; sometimes it feels sad – but then, when I'm writing, I feel fiendishly good. About writing as an act I feel good, and even about some of my writing as a product; it's the question of writing as a profession that makes me tremble and shake, and look furtive when people ask me what I do, and hide behind my children and my part-time teaching. I don't think any act of will or 'change of attitude' on my part can alter that: I won't have any public confidence about my writing until I've published more. But I won't stop writing – I wouldn't stop writing unless I stopped thinking of things to write. That's a fate that seems much worse to contemplate than my present limbo.

Chapter 3

A FEMINIST WRITER'S PROGRESS

Sara Maitland

Once upon a time (it was in 1950) a little girl was born. When she was growing up she wanted to be a writer. (At least she wanted to be a writer most of the time: some of the time she wanted to be a farmer, a classical philologist, married to Prince Charles, an explorer, a barrister, a lock-keeper, a boy, an actress, the mistress of an eighteenth-century salon, an accident victim, a nun and various other similar avocations.) As she was an imaginative child with a precocious grasp of words, being a writer was one of the few ambitions which her family felt able to encourage. They also, luckily for her, believed very strongly in Education and saw that she got lots of it, both the formal sort acquired at excellent if startlingly dull girls' private schools, and more generally a diffused sense of Western Culture. Her mother felt that she herself had been deprived of such an education and was anxious for her girl children to have it; her father felt that Western Culture belonged to him – not exclusively, but to him and his kind as the direct heirs of the classical era via the Renais-sance – and he gave it as a gift to all his children, as unself-consciously but determinedly as he gave them other good things like food and clothes. So successful were her family in this project that it took the little girl years to understand what other women meant when they said they had been excluded from mainstream culture.

Now all this was very nice for the little girl, but as a writer she had a problem. She had no subject matter. Intro-version was severely discouraged as morbid in her home so that it never occurred to her to write very directly about her interior life. And all the other good stories had already been told: by the Greeks, by the Gospel writers, by Chaucer and

Shakespeare, by the Whig historians and by the nineteenth-century novelists. It certainly was a problem.

Well, inevitably the little girl grew up and she went to a University with ancient pale towers and lots of young oppressed poets. In her first year there she learned a number of very important things: that she was not cut out to be an academic; that her commitment to stories and her class background would stop her being like the other young poets; that she was profoundly confused and unhappy; that politics mattered; that being mad was not any fun at all; and that men were more boring and more mean than she had been hoping. These discoveries, while all immensely useful, ruled out all her other ambitions and did not solve the problem of having no subject matter.

Then later the little girl got lucky. Do you remember the story of Cinderella? She is sitting at home rather pissed off, wanting to go to the ball and not having a thing to wear, when the fairy godmother whizzes in and puts it all right. One of the important things about the fairy godmother is that she transforms all the old stuff around Cinderella into new and useful equipment: the rags, the pumpkin, the rats and so forth. This little girl's fairy godmother turned out to be called Feminism. As well as cheering the little girl up no end Feminism also transformed all the old things around her. Above all (in this context) she transformed the old stories. Suddenly the little girl could see that the stories were just vehicles; they had been told over and over again for different purposes and could be told one more time at least; they could be told through brand new shining feminist eyes. What excitement. Quickly the little girl realised that there were enormous advantages to using old stories: everyone knew them so the narrative could be stripped right down (saving lots of time) and they were filled with the reverberations of everyone's dreams; because there needed to be so little machinery it was easier to dive deep into them and find their rhythms; and especially the little girl knew them very well (or so she thought at the time) and could live happily inside them and not get lost in the forest. Immediately the little girl thanked the fairy godmother, being well brought up, and set out on her quest to become a Feminist Writer.

Now we stop calling her the little girl.

Now we learn that identifying the quest is the beginning not the end.

The first obstacle that the Feminist Writer had to negotiate, and indeed has to renegotiate over and over again, was a narrow passage between two grinding rocks. This is a dangerous crossing and littered with the bones of would-be feminist writers who never made it through. On the one hand the feminist writer could hear all her old education and all her old artistic friends, and her own old artistic consciousness booming out that politics and great writing cannot go together; that gender and imagination are enemies not friends; that Virginia Woolf (who is constantly dragged in here, her hair still dripping from the river) herself had said that the writer has to be androgynous. Inspiration, these voices hissed at her, will not be held captive to a theory, to an isolated vision, to a message. Feminism, though all very nice in its own way, could not be a Universal, a proper Cultural Voice. Feminism cannot be Art.

And on the other side, close and deadly, the other feminists – and the right-on loyal feminist in her own gut, who knew what she had been given and wanted conscientiously to pay her debts – sucked and pulled at her hands and snapped out that what she was writing was not 'good feminism', was not 'useful to ordinary women', gave too much away to the enemy, and did not show the glories of our womanly souls.

Do you know much about quest literature? For the quest to be successfully accomplished various things are needful. One, of course, is courage and constancy and intelligence and flexibility and attentiveness on the part of the questor (oh dear, oh dear. That's the hard bit really). But there are other necessities. And one of these is finding companions. Well, the Feminist Writer floundered between these two ever-shifting rocks for some years, sometimes making progress, sometimes simply holding her ground and sometimes getting sucked up by one side or the other. Then she found some companions and some companionship in that place. Because it is rather important their names shall be listed without allegorical diversion: Zoe Fairbairns, Valerie Miner, Michele Roberts and Michelene Wandor. And the five of them formed a Feminist Writers' Group and they made a book[1] together and they made so much noise between them that they no longer heard the crashing voices. Once they had escaped from that trap, do you know that they found that it was perfectly obvious that both sides were liars and there was plenty of room to pass safely between them? The memory and voices of that obstacle often returned to haunt the Feminist Writer, but basically she had learned that the voices were just her own excuses and had to be forcibly ignored. And she had also learned that being a Feminist Writer is not meant to be a lonely and isolated business, because she did not just want companions on her quest, she actually needed them. So that was good.

And passing between the two rocks, unscathed and considerably strengthened with confidence and companionship, our Feminist Writer came out onto a sweet plain where she lived for a few years. She wrote a number of short stories and some of them were published and even read. She wrote a novel[2] and a book about being a Christian Feminist[3] and some articles and essays and reviews. She frolicked quite a lot and was patted on the head a bit and criticised too. Now these things were not all easy to do and they cost her quite a lot of effort and innocence and they raised questions in her mind, but by and large it was a good time for her. In all the quests there are these good times and in all the quests they come to a sticky end. Indeed, as the Feminist Writer proceeded on her way the going got rougher. She knew, despite the playing and working with other things, what her own quest really was: to re-tell the old stories again and fill in some bits that got left out. She knew what her own form was too – the intense and even constraining space of the short story, vibrating with the voices of tradition and memory, which could uniquely force the emotions she wanted to explore down into her own vulnerable places, and thence she hoped into the vulnerable places of other women. The other writings developed her muscle and fed her face (and sometimes distracted and sometimes helped her) but most of all she wanted to write more stories and more stories and more stories because this was her quest.

But the stories got darker. At first the Feminist Writer had written morally uplifting tales like how Hippolyta, the Amazon Queen, influenced Theseus, the classical hero, for good; and how Pope Joan despised her own worldly success; and how Penelope was not the sucker you might take her for; and as for Mary Magdalen, well, 'what a friend she had in Jesus'. In her stories at the beginning of the quest women-in-struggle were the goodies and men were the baddies – except possibly under tender-but-true feminist guidance when they might have a chance of redemption. But soon the Feminist Writer found out a number of disconcerting things. When she wrote about women and wrote truly out of her own experience of herself as a woman she had to recognise the conniving, treacherous, unloving, unlovely things that she did. And these killings and betrayals and cruelties and stupidities were all there in the stories and could not be escaped. Cassandra was crazed and Clytemnestra lethal; Jael was bloodthirsty and Delilah treacherous. Women chop up their babies and sell each other down the river. The Goddesses side with men and women betray their sisters and their mothers and their daughters. Women-in-struggle are incarcerated, mutilated and massacred and do not live to tell the tale. Women choose madness and badness daily and mythologically, and the Feminist Writer could not go on with her quest without telling these stories too. This became very difficult. It was not just that people did not like her stories, though more and more women would look up in the middle and say that they were unreadable in their extremity (and this hurt her), but the stories were beginning to scare her too. This was not an obstacle like the other one, external and possible; this was more like rolling an ever-heavier stone up an ever-steepening hill, and the Feminist Writer did not find it any fun. Because she had abandoned Social Realism as the best or only way to speak the truth she often found that she no longer had the balancing pole of simple probability to protect her. There were no natural limits. She was afraid. She was afraid that the stone, so weighty, so carefully poised, would start to slip backwards and crush her, and she would be squashed quite flat by the images inside her head. It was impossible just to ignore the stone or let it roll off wherever it would, but

the danger of being flattened scared her badly. Very badly
sometimes.

Do you remember the bit earlier on about things that are
needed on a good quest? Well, along with companions there is
another common aid for the questing heroine – the wise
animal. What happens is that the person on the quest diverts
briefly to help some animal out of some natural difficulty
(thorns in feet seem to crop up rather frequently). In
exchange for this good-will or casual act of love the animal
turns up again later in the quest and returns the compliment.
Now earlier in the story and quite by chance (which is why it
got forgotten at the right time) the Feminist Writer had
acquired a wise animal of her own. She had had a baby
daughter. Most of her companions on this sort of quest seem
to have found babies, whatever other joys they may bring
with them, to be major and serious distractions. But our
Feminist Writer found that when confronting the danger of
being flattened, pushed under, destroyed or something like
that by her heavy stone, the daughter turned out to have
the answer. Just what was needed. The practical demands
that the child made, the necessity of meeting them, their
inescapable dailiness and unavoidableness, the definitive
Social Realism of them created exactly the balance that could
save her. However deep she was pushed into the muddy
darkness by the weight of the rocky images and heavy truths
she would have to come out again because the daughter
would be there demanding fish fingers and attention. In the
depth of the labyrinth, with the greedy-mouthed monster
ready to pounce, the thread would be tugged firmly and she
would wind it into a tidy little ball and come on out. The
daughter (and later as it happens the Feminist Writer had
another baby, a son this time, who, though more of a domestic
pet than a wise animal, performed the same function) was
like a stout pillar to which the kite string can be tied so that it
will not fly away, and the Feminist Writer felt safer. What is
more, having got into the habit of letting the daughter keep
her safe, she learned to trust other guides and guardians too.
So now she had excellent companions and peers on her quest,
and also had practically a zoo of wise animals, ancient crones,
gurus, witches and sibyls. And all of these helped her a lot, as

they always do on quests, and though the stone stayed heavy and the road stayed steep, it did not all seem totally impossible.

(Sometimes the Feminist Writer felt a bit ashamed of needing all these outside props and aids, because she would have liked to be a Strong Woman, but one day she went to the Circus and saw a tight-rope walker; and on the programme was a note which said 'Anyone who would perform without a safety-net is either suicidal or stupid.' So she thanked the Feminist tight-rope walker, being well brought up, and went on her way rejoicing.)

Now apologies are due. This questing tale is a bit of a con, because it is too soon to say what happened to our Feminist Writer in the end. Whether or not she achieved her quest and wrote beautiful stories (and even other things too) that moved herself and other women to understand more what they were about and what to do about it; whether she learned to shed her fear and climb boldly and lovingly over or round or through the next set of obstacles never mind the ones beyond and the ones beyond that; whether she stuck with her quest to the very end and so mapped out new territories where other questing women could go and write new stories; whether she did succeed in taking back even a few of the old stories and telling them anew so that they became ours; whether she got right into the middle of women's silence *and* came back *and* found words for what she found there; and whether the trumpets sounded for her on the other side – all these things are not yet known. This is the beginning of the story only.[4,5]

SOME NOTES

1 This book was called *Tales I Tell my Mother* (Journeyman Press, 1978).
2 The novel was *Daughter of Jerusalem* (Blond & Briggs, 1978).
3 *A Map of the New Country* (Routledge & Kegan Paul, 1983).
4 You will have to work out the meanings and morals of this story for yourself.
5 Whether, and in what ways, you believe any of this is, of course, entirely up to you, but remember always that the writer is a writer of fictions and too literal or chronological a belief may prove dangerous to your health.

Chapter 4

THE ERRANT UNICORN
Judith Kazantzis

A conceited start; bear with me. I have a point, if a perverse one. After two collections of poetry I suspect I may now have a modest name as a feminist poet. I suspect – or rather I fear – well, heaven knows it is nice to be liked, very nice, and warming to feel my poetry has got itself a social context, a place however minute in the tramp tramp of the times.

But I do fear also the adjective, like a lovely convolvulus, entrapping the still fragile noun. I prefer to call myself poet and feminist (or vice versa) – political commitment, as Orwell suggests in *Inside the Whale*, can kill creative impulse. This impulse – in me, as in many – is perverse, erratic, and hates to be named, thus stereotyped (after all, it was in protest against the great patriarchal stereotypes that I became a feminist). I often feel I must protect the impulse from my own tendency to tight rein it in intellectual argumentation, I must allow it to wander, even if it chooses – oh horror – to wander off the ideological straight of feminism. What if my poetry should express that blasphemy, dislike of women; consciously, or worse, unconsciously: so that I didn't even see it till I'm hauled in for questioning. Surprising how many other feminists who write are terrorised by this possibility as well as myself – patriarchal mother at it again.

Also I often feel quite the opposite: I must seize this errant unicorn that I struggle with somewhere at the back of my head; and ride it hard in the direction that my feminism, my anti-militarism, my anti-Establishment left idealism wants to go. For I do believe a poet who is on the left should write to change her/his society; I try from time to time to frame explicit political comment, to take on the challenge of making poetry for 'the people'. Parenthesis: Oh, oh, who are the people? Mr and Mrs Bloggs, Master and Miss Bloggs, that happy manual family my school education taught me was 'the people'? In this mixed-up society, could be anyone – lovers or likers of poetry are as random as inspiration. But I guess for myself a reader, probably female, between 30 and 50, already attuned to modern poetry (my poetry has been described as 'difficult' – I too have been described as difficult – I don't see it). A reader therefore not necessarily a self-named feminist but who still relates to my particular brand of protest.

But this is a simple monolithic ghost. Really, I write for myself, with an eye to the whole world. Ho hum. . . . My worldly yet high-minded father brought me up to be both a proselytiser and a democrat. Fishy? The fact is I can't have it all ways, I am no curly-haired angel-faced male poet who can write worse verse for the masses and better verse for the clientele all at once and sell lots – Well, genuine secret ambition: I'd like to be able to write radical lyrics, and sing them even. (Guildenstern playing the watchman?) Dammit, I can neither play nor sing. . . . Parenthesis ends.

Political comment means rhetoric and satire, by and large (it doesn't have to). Yet on the other tack, lyric poetry, private poetry, and the great personal themes of death, of love, of lack of love, have a greater traditional pull for a poet, certainly in this country. It is obvious that a personal poem of a non-topical quality can mean more in the end to more people than the most brilliant piece of topical argumentation. Which tack, as a poet and a feminist, should I adopt?

I enjoy satire but I find that temperamentally I look inwards, so that usually (like most verse writers) I write poems of private record and fantasy. If this goes on too long I get worried at my solipsism – for one thing it can run so thin. But the old feminist saying 'the personal is the political' comforts me in general.

Though I would not claim, nor wish to claim, that the more personal poems I write are all grounded in high feminism. Some are about country life, and I send them to *Country Life*, others are about fucking and possibly sexist and these I might send to male editors and gauchely assume that *Spare Rib* readers – for whom I have reviewed women's poetry for some years – won't come across them. Back, however, to Orwell. Toeing an ideological line can have the writer of imagination lock herself into a 'constipating little cage of lies' in the end. So that is why I prefer to be a feminist and a poet, rather than. . . .

As for the problem of the private poem versus the public, the real answer is a fusion of the two; this is the sort of poetry I want to write: where topical events can be allied without falsity to my own inner life and both can mirror something more universal. (How every poet strives to write something universal! Come back in, great marvellous Blake.)

Having fought off the stereotype, I acknowledge willingly that I owe much of my poetic drive to feminist anger or despair. I was married early in the 1960s, had two small children, continuous bad health and no real career. I found myself depressed and housebound. As soon as I read about the Women's Movement, circa 1970–1, I joined it – in a vague but convinced way. Betty Friedan had long revealed to me that I was aching from the ill of the feminine mystique and I had myself contributed a 'Jackdaw' (a students' history kit) in 1968 on women's emancipation: 'Women in Revolt', a drop added to the new medicines of self-exploration and self-discovery.

I put in work for the first Women's Liberation Workshop, in Earlham Street, in London. I was also painting continuously and wanted to be a painter. But from 1973 painting gradually moved over for writing – poetry, more and more of it, after I had had a massive word-rich injection of Sylvia Plath one wintry week in February of that year. (Ten years since she died.)

The first poem I wrote – I had written perhaps five poems since university days, though until I was twenty-one I wrote steadily – was a chancy, glancing, rhythmically rather clumsy attack on my mother. My early poetry was full of psychoanalytic tryouts; angry monologues, parts of selves speaking, Laingian weed-garden ghosts, bobbing up again, all of it aimed at freeing myself from old dependencies: a painful yet invaluable use of poetry I found other feminists were making. In the course of this I began to write some good poems.

How has being a mother myself affected my poetry? Directly I have written only a very few poems about my two children; each I remember as important to me. I struggled intimately with them just as I have struggled to respond to my children, with success and with failure. The total experience, the uneasy self-identification with motherhood, the domestic prison nest has come into many poems. My first collection was called *Minefield*; the title poem was about my own relationship to my mother. As a whole the book seems to me to breathe imprisonment in mother/family stereotypes, and the violent clumsy effort to break free of this double-yolked egg, the yolk of my own childhood, the yolk of my own motherhood. What a double word! A twice yolk that fed me many riches, yet constrained me, halved my own potential.

I joined the Women's Movement essentially to make closer friends with other women – whom I had feared as fantasy rivals, whom I now wished to work with as fellow detainees out to free ourselves. This wish was both met and tested in the feminist writers' group to which I belonged throughout the 1970s. The argument that has enriched and weakened the movement, enriched and weakened this group. I mean the old conundrum that dwindles so often into: are all males total pigs or are some less piggish than others? The interesting question – can men be lived with, privately, publicly – became (for me) the persecutory question: *should* men be lived with; with its persecutory refrain – No! I experienced all the heat and sterility of this separatist/non-separatist argument. Underneath, the fruitful life went on, all of us sorting out our own life views. But this liveliness began to feel like the rolling of tanks up through opposing trench systems, so little tolerance at times seemed on offer to the other side. Meanwhile, whole areas of discussion slid under the grinding of the tank treads. Ironically, it was affection and shared idealism that heated this intolerance. Nostalgia bound us to our sterile efforts to find again the old enthusiastic unity, the 'Bliss was it in that dawn' feeling of the early 1970s.

I have been in other writing groups, mixed and women only, and find satisfaction in more limited goals now, like putting together a poetry manuscript over a specified time –

the emotional heights of feminist group life seem ringed to me now with a litterland of objects thrown. My theme here is rooted, I suddenly see, in that long, rich but troubling group experience; which often supported me (and I gave too) but from which I sometimes emerged feeling clobbered and less feminist than thou.

Yet if that particular reality was not easy for me, it did not stop my writing about women, and probably encouraged it. More and more, as the poems got written I found they were about women; especially women in myth, fairy tale or drama. I wrote on Cinderella, on Bluebeard's Fatima, on Little Red Riding Hood. Turning for information to Robert Graves's wonderful *Greek Myths* and remembering back to a childhood of Nathaniel Hawthorne's *Tanglewood Tales*, I wrote on Penelope, Circe, Europa, and at most length on Clytemnestra. Clytemnestra fascinated me – she, the archetypal wicked queen: what was *her* story? I tried to tell the most famous murder in myth from the murderess's point of view. I wanted to show Clytemnestra not as a crazy bitch but as a human being with both strong passions and good reasons. I did not want to idealise her either. In my writers' group experience I was learning the same ancient truism, synthesised of patriarchal thought and feminist feeling. Women are neither all bad nor all good, but human . . . me included.

Deeply I was out to expunge from myself an ex-Catholic's sense of damnation – something horribly embedded in me. It has, I realised, been since adolescence depressingly entwined with a sense of somehow not being 'womanly', 'attractive': hence a linked revolt in me, against the patriarchal mores which has defined and too easily has damned women, and against God, that old whitebeard who is after all a giant star, a male projection. Cruel and aloof, God does seem a rich myth figure through which to have at patriarchal arrogance – recently I have written several pieces about *Him*!

And in others I have tried to satirise or to speak about the nuclear danger in which men (not, I do believe, women, when all is said and done) have placed our planet. Aware of the dangers of this kind of polarisation for a feminist (and an egalitarian), I still think it undeniable that women are the gentler, more loving sex, *pace* Margaret Thatcher and the imitation men. If we had more belief in ourselves! I do not think that if women ran the world it could be in more danger! But I know that is a both soppy and academic (e.g. ridiculously incontestable) point of view.

Generally I enjoy writing poems making mock of men and their plaguing ways. Over the years I have been tending to grow mildly coarser (language carefully – ah, Eng. Lit. – *couched* in elegant syntax; but maybe I am jogging freer of that too).

This has frightened me in advance when I come to plan readings. 'Cunt/vagina' worry me outside London – even in London – dare I read some poem which playfully hints at damage to the 'prick/penis'? (I think 'penis' is held more sacred, i.e. harder to say publicly than 'vagina'.) Ladylike this may sound to free spirits but –

I dare: I come, I see the audience, I dare and so far I've not been thumped or had my mouth washed out by the jolly vicar. On the contrary I conclude that the most enjoyable poems for a feminist to read to a mixed audience are often the most provocative, as long as there's a laugh around. Men can, alas, take a lot.

I have occasionally been just as stymied reading to all-feminist audiences: heterosexual love poems in which the words 'penis' or 'prick' again for different reasons present difficulties – fear that separatist women will dislike it – have reluctantly been given the boot. Oh well, back I go to older poems, more full of reinstated harpies, furies and miseries over motherhood. (But prefer, truly, to choose happier poems.)

This sort of mild trimming (which we all do, except the utterly pure of heart who never travel abroad anyway) sometimes makes me wonder how much longer I shall be labelled a feminist poet. The fact is I have no idea where my errant poetry, whatever it is, will take me now. I do know it, like me, will always want to make fun of the isms and the ologies. The solemnity of feminist sisterhood, particularly the Goddess lot, is a colourful target: the annoyingness of some types of women ditto however caused – and more intimately known to me personally than, say, the horrors of rape, therefore easier to describe. In my poking fun must I never sting women?

Must I stick to pig-sticking men? Difficult one. I say my prayers to the Goddess.

To be honest to myself my verse must follow my life. Therefore when I am in love, so I write besotted love poems. When I and the man split up, I write miserable, lorn, angry poetry – and have a great increase in insight into what other bereft women feel about men's hardness.

This may be very erratic and reprehensible by my own fixed philosophical principles but one thing is obvious to me: I can only write into life what is real; impossible to write against the grain of my continuing experiences. To me it is always a bit of a surprise that I can write a poem at all – that it becomes created. It is a precious reminder to myself that I live, that I have senses and an intellect and an art. Therefore I must protect my poetry against outside demands.

On the other hand, as Orwell suggested somewhere, only fools think you can write without a subject . . . and that includes poetry. I must say something I want to repeat to others. If it is only about my solipsistic sensuous progress, joyful and sad, to the grave, that is good – better still if I can write in a way which gives other people and especially women a sense of pride and of closeness.

Chapter 5

NOTES ON WRITING
A Marxist/Feminist Viewpoint
Wendy Mulford

the work is
e.g. to write 'she' and for that to be a statement
of fact only and not a strong image
of everything which is not-you, which sees you.[1]

'Communism . . . is only the beginning' (Harry McShane).

I've been writing for about twelve years, running a small press, Street Editions, and for eight years I've been in the Communist Party and been an increasingly bloody-minded feminist. I find it hard to estimate exactly what has happened to my writing in this period, but certainly at the outset I found it impossible to value what I was doing – to see it at all clearly. It just seemed to dribble out. Out of the intensity of my feeling, I think I would have said. I started to discover what I was doing about 1974–5, at the time that I was publishing some key 'modernist' texts by contemporaries and when I hadn't yet published anything myself except in magazines. I started to find out through my involvement in the women's movement, and my friendships with particular women. That was the time when the whole question of the 'construction' of the self started to form mistily on the skyline. Who was this 'I' speaking? What was speaking me? How far did the illusion of selfhood, that most intimate and precious possession, reach? How could the lie of culture be broken up if the lie of the self made by that culture remained intact? And how could the lie of capitalist society be broken if the lie of culture were not broken?

'I insist on positing certain things . . . precisely because I engage myself.'[2] The engagement for me, personally, over the last three years has been in my writing to counter the

31

particular lie of the universal transcendent nature of art and of art's function to 'coax on stage'[3] the truth known already elsewhere, in which art acts as confirmation of knowledge we possess by other means, representation of enduring human truth. I have been concerned to *produce* meaning *across* and in defiance of the repressive codes of everyday, communication-ready language. I haven't been concerned directly with either expression or representation of meaning, although I would not go so far as to say I have had *no* 'relation of obligation to the law of legibility'.[4] I have attempted to make myself open to language itself, to allow language to enter in and claim the field of writing, rather than seeking to make language my tool. To use desire as the fuel at the face of language itself, in the play of the unconscious, producing meaning that can then not be reappropriated into the discourse of the known. (To speak directly against the repressions, the deformities of our history with the tongue, the voice of unmediated desire, to shout rebellion against the cabining of human energy by the categories of Law, violating that Law through *speech*. AUDIBLE SOUND. SHOUTS IN THE THROAT OF TOMORROW.)

It's clear that certain fairly familiar areas of discussion have been crudely raided here for this schematic account of my position as a writer – and I'd like to emphasise that I don't imagine or wish to further the debates about language and the construction of self in *theoretical* terms in my writing.[5] If I write inevitably from the place of being an 'intellectual' through my education and profession, that place is shot through with arrows of resistance and doubt, unease and disbelief. It is a place of recalcitrance. Polemically I insist with other women critics against the majority of left male criticism that gender and class *are* equally-weighted determinants of any literary production. Polemically I insist with other modernist writers against the practice of most women that for the writer revolutionary practice necessitates revolutionary practice in the field of the signifier. Two sets of agreements, two sets of disagreements. Place of intersection. + How central that looks. But how few people these agreements and disagreements reach!

What does reach many people, many women, is the *reach*

of difference. It's barely credible that even now the hegemony of one sex of one class of one race should be so deep that it can still pass for the universal experience of our culture, that in most places there's not even the question, a problematic of the discourse for people not of this category. As Marxist/Feminists our work has surely to be in speaking that difference, challenging the assumptions and the constraints, the ideological categories, the metaphorical configurations, the syntax of subordination, pressing against the constructs 'man woman', 'child parent', 'family sexuality' – 'flying in the face/of what is called natural'.[6] There will be, there must be, of course, many different ways of doing this. I want to look briefly at some of the problems I've met in attempting to work at the 'language-face'.

The first problem is one of isolation. My writing is read and heard mainly by men engaged in poetic practices of differing kinds for whom my work has significance because of the attempt I have been making to work at the level of the production of meaning. But I want to join my voice with the voices of other *women* struggling to destruct the lie of culture.

Contemporary experimental Marxist/Feminist writing is also untouched by the critical activity of those Marxist/Feminists best placed to understand it, whose work in related theoretical areas on the symbolic and the construction of the subject, for example, is directed towards the mainstream, nineteenth- and early twentieth-century texts of the 'great tradition' taught in universities. And many of them don't care to read contemporary writing, unless it is offering representations of women today in a positive way. I may be being less than wholly fair here but it does seem to me that there's a remarkable absence of cross-fertilisation between women working in the theoretical field and those producing certain kinds of contemporary fiction and poetry, both here and in America, a cross-fertilisation which I for one would very much welcome.

The second problem is the difficulty of the task itself, of engaging as poet with the materiality of language. If language is the crucial signifying practice in and through which the human subject is constructed and becomes a social human being, the question for the woman writer appears to

be how can she through her writing subvert that language
which is the instrument of the Law? What *in practice* does it
mean for her to talk about the revolutionary violation of the
Law? What is its potential for the 'transformation of the
actual world'? Some women have argued that the first act
must be to remake language itself.

Yes, we must break through our silence. But we cannot
create a language. We can make a lexical selection, designed
to exclude, for example, the obvious phallic metaphors of
penetration, thrust, etc., for forceful action, for energy and
desire. Such a lexical pruning and substitution of new items
(such as chairperson) is part of the process of *thinking* our
language, realising its subtle articulations of male dominance, making some redress and calling the female into
presence in verbs, qualifiers, substantives and pronouns.

But this is a small linguistic process. It doesn't even
touch on the implication of syntax – the compound-complex
structure of sentences, with its main and dependent clauses
carefully balanced, the logical tendency of our linear-
directed language that makes it impossible to think across
structures of main and subordinate intention, categories
of negative/positive and binary logic. And it doesn't touch
on language as the shaping reality in our *past*: that
social and historical reality in and through which we have
been assigned our social and personal identities since in-
fancy. We cannot choose to assume or dismiss language at
will.

The third problem relates to the date on the calendar and
the modernist or neo-modernist tradition within which I see
my work as located. Contemporary male writers write from a
clear sense of place defined by the work of previous writers in
the modernist tradition, of Mallarmé, Rimbaud, Tzara,
Artaud, for example. But for me there is always a barrier, a
sense of 'otherness' about this tradition. As one poet put it to
me, 'it must be as if you are on the other side of a huge sheet of
plate glass', and I think I would agree. Clearly there's no
question of writing as if 'Un coup de dés n'abolira jamais le
hasard' (a throw of the dice will never abolish chance) had
never been written, but equally I can't *assume* that work, for
it was produced from a differently gendered place. I have, as

it were, only a colonial relationship to such texts inhabiting a language and a culture which I'm not quite at ease in, which doesn't quite fit. This problem is obviously keyed into the previous one of language itself, but it has a slightly different area of impact for it's particularly in *reading* that I'm made aware of it. I can't stay only with the work of poets and writers such as Anne Waldman, Kathy Acker or Alice Notley for it becomes like the Borgia torture, the chamber whose walls close in closer and closer till you suffocate. There simply isn't enough work, and the major breakthroughs have been made by men. But turning to that work, my sense of alienation (Alice James, what happened to Rimbaud's sister . . .) bounces me back again. At some times this tension is creative, but often it is merely frustrating and I become impatient.

In conclusion I want to say something about the concepts (?) 'Poet', 'Poem' and 'Poetic Tradition'. I think these concepts need to be seriously challenged and de-fetishised. They are not rooted in the objective relations of our society and they encourage and prop up the idea of this art as a magical art, which must be performed by elite beings-apart. The prevalence of these notions in poetry, and the failure to challenge them, is a very real indication of the problem facing high art in a capitalist society – how its practice is tied into and legitimated by society precisely because in its hierarchical and elite nature it *reinforces* the ideological hierarchy of aspiration and remains the property of the few. I'd suggest that men can use these concepts in support of their particular artistic practice (even when in other ways the implications of what they do point in quite another direction) because they can still more easily be spokesmen of their culture, culture which because of gender is never ours in the same way, even though because of class it is not theirs either, and they/you too are working to 'deconstruct' it, to take it apart.

In my head as I write are the reverberations of other parts of struggle, of other kinds of consciousness; my place in the family, sounds of children's voices, of work, of politics, shifts in sexuality and relationships, leading into and out of the house, 'home', and how we live. Small, material, local, *domestic*. The centre of our politics. Ten years ago I would have seen that as triviality, not reaching the important, universal conditions. Now I see these material conditions as the reality within which we work. Perhaps some people will see what I have said in its emphasis on the specificity of women's struggle and women's place as divisive, but I think in order to transform society from this inhumane, partial, literally murderous state we have to recognise first that material reality, to see laser-sharp how it is structured at its deepest level on the sexual divide in order to be able to work together, as men and women, to change it, a task as urgent for artists as for workers in any other field.

If this comes across as a gloomy picture I think the task in poetry is harder than in other areas of artistic practice. Poetry has traditionally been a minority high-art pursuit and the problems of isolation and fragmentation are most acute here. Even where materials and forms are crude as yet, the coming together of women to create art in many different ways, and the breaking down of the artist–audience divide, together with experimentation, constitute the opening up of a real challenge to the dominant culture.

(Red Letters, No 9, 1979)

NOTES

1 Denise Riley, 'A note on sex and the reclaiming of language', *Marxism for Infants*, Street Editions, 1977.
2 Helene Cixous, interview with Christiane Makward, *Substance*, no. 13, 1976.
3 David Trotter, contrasting officially-approved, mainstream poetry, which uses traditional expressive and representational modes of writing with the 'transcursive' writing of the New Poetries in 'Matter for Thought', 'The New Poetries' in *P. N. Review*, vol. 5, no. 3.
4 Cixous, *op. cit.*
5 But see Denise Riley, *Marxism for Infants*, Street Editions, 1977, *No Fee* (with W. M.), 1979.
6 Michele Roberts, 'Caterpillar', in *Cutlasses & Earrings*, London, 1977.

THREE YEARS ON (1982)

When I sat down to write this, I thought I was going to pick up from the above, and talk about the problems of writing as a woman and as a modernist poet. Instead I found myself writing angrily, desperately, about survival and what possible place women writers could have at this present juncture, how we could use our voices to help build resistance to the threat of nuclear genocide. Since that is what I care about most today, what I originally intended to talk about, my personal shaping as a woman and as a writer doesn't any longer seem terribly interesting, or relevant.

I don't mean that everything besides 'The Bomb', as we used to call it in the 1960s, before MAD or Preemptive Strike existed 'for our protection' – I'll drop the quotation marks here before they drown the rest of what I'm going to say – falls away into a bland and unimportant backcloth. On the contrary. Class and gender difference divide us as sharply now as they ever did, and in our daily experience we know all too accurately the poverty and powerlessness of our condition. At the same time, we also know our strength, how we support each other, how we fight for a decent wage for our health workers, fight to stop our schools being closed, how we protest at our jobs being taken and at the assertions of an economy too poor to provide basic social necessities for its people when the arms bill swells flagrantly every week. And we know the elation and deepening of our resolve to resist that comes from every shared action.

But it is not clear to me how that struggle in its local and daily reality relates now to our situation, on the brink of not-being, and particularly how it relates for feminist writers. How do we understand this as present reality, that unless we achieve a major transformation, unless we can coerce our leaders into reversing their policy of accelerating nuclear accumulation, we face the almost certain destruction of a large part of our world and its civilisation within the next few years? How can we be alive in language to an imagined reality so huge, so careless and wanton, it assumes not just our individual death – hard enough to encompass – but the virtual death of the planet? What would a feminist poetics and practice be that was strong enough to take on such a challenge?

I think that's an important question to ask, even though it's unanswerable. What I am thinking of is not the kind of poetry that 'services' the women's or any other movement, not words for marching songs and hallelujahs for meeting-halls, though we need those too (and ballads, satires, odes, lyrics, epigrams, pop lyrics, choruses, and, and), but poetry that is *transformative*, that compels us to recognitions we would prefer not to see, and makes us aware of choices we had denied:

> When we become acutely, disturbingly aware of the language we are using and *that is using us* (my italics) we begin to grasp a material resource that women have never before collectively attempted to repossess . . . as long as our language is inadequate, our vision remains formless, our thinking and feeling are still running in the old cycles, our process may be revolutionary but not transformative. ('Power and Danger: Works of a Common Woman', in Adrienne Rich, *On Lies, Secrets and Silence*, 1979.)

It takes so long for transformation to occur in ourselves and the processes of transformation are continuous, at every level. For myself I can trace those processes back through class, family and gender struggles, as a child and adolescent in Wales, as a student and young married woman in Cambridge, later as a poet and teacher in London. My fight to discover my independent self as a woman is enmeshed in my mind with my fight to believe in my voice as a poet. That fight was supported by my mother who, as a cellist, had when she was young refused the narrow construction of female identity of her class, by my teachers in Wales, by menfriends who were poets, and, contradictorily, not necessarily knowingly, by the two men I married. My English teachers at Cambridge did not, I think, aid that process – and they certainly made it difficult for me to write with any confidence for many years.

The greatest processes of transformation occurred for me through the Women's Liberation Movement, which changed, little by little, so much of my life, my teaching, my writing, my friendships, relationships with men and women; it's impossible to measure the reach of it. My feeling is that the peace movement has to grow to be such a matrix, that is, that we have to work to make it grow to such a reach, such a depth. But as women we experience oppression in different ways daily; the nuclear threat, while a present threat, is not for many people a present reality. We have to imagine our deaths, and as I have said, that is almost impossible to do, precisely because we are so committed to our lives.

For myself, I was a teacher until quite recently and my decision to give up teaching was influenced by my sense of the urgency of this present moment, that I must work and write where I can wholly commit myself. My writing, however, still works restlessly within the unreconstructed domain of the passions. This implies for me continuing to work with a subject, and 'I', despite or through its rifts, absences, contradictions, yet an 'I' which carries links with the Coleridgean 'I' in its perception of itself as moral agent and as in part imaginative creator of its world. Corkscrewing between this space of the 'I' and the actual world is that force we call love, creating its desired visionary world, in a relentless twisting to and fro of energy I map as a triangle. And what is transformative for me in this traditional mapping, even in our contemporary bleakness, is 'I' as active and desiring subject, that 'I' being specifically gendered.

Where libidinal energy and social determination are cathected in the poem to create, at the deepest level, a passionate utterance of the will to love, it may be that we can move, both men and women to resistance, resistance constructed on our woman-knowledge and our refusal of the politics of death. Rarely, but occasionally, poetry has moved me in that way. Poetry by Denise Levertov, for example, or Adrienne Rich. Moving us to speech, which itself is action, but further, into action we have not yet dreamed of, prefigured maybe in the coming together of women at Greenham Common, and other peace camps. In one year the women at Greenham have changed that name from the sign of a missile base to the sign of peace. That is real change, based on numbers of transformations occurring throughout that year.

Three years ago I wrote of the small, local and domestic

struggles whose sounds reverberated in my ears from elsewhere, from other parts of life, as I wrestled to fuse together
the apparently contradictory practices of a modernist poetics
and a Marxist/Feminist politics. Now I am no longer sure of
the place of these struggles. I do not know if my daughter will
live to be twenty or I fifty or you to your next decade, and
there is no texture to this new, unknown knowledge. It is
leeched of all colour and shape. I have to live each day as if it
were the only one and you not here and each dawn precious.

And yet, of course, looking into my sunlit familiar
garden in its green stragglyness, it is possible to believe only
in the reality of now, to occlude our general death. I must
disbelieve a murderous future continuously being manu-
factured daily in our present, it is too gross to believe. We sit
typing, drinking tea, laughing, talking with our children, our
friends and lovers, making cakes, delivering notices. Surely
only that is real. . . . And I continue to write poems, passionately concerned with desire and imagination, with my search
for you, the Other, that absence in whose features are com-
posed all the specificity of the beloved, Woman, the highest
condition to which I may aspire . . . and I watch the old ladies
swaying slightly down the street, their knees buckling under
the weight of shopping . . . and I listen to my neighbours in
the corner butcher's discussing the latest rape attack in our
neighbourhood and my blood runs cold to hear them laugh
and say 'ah, you should've been so lucky, Maudie, you'd've
liked it right enough if it been you', and I have no answers.

As feminists we know how our personal and our wider
political commitments are inextricably bound up, how we
unblock our power and share our energy, how we become
freer and more powerful through our sharing. We also know
what an acutely reactionary concentration of power we face
in the ruling male capitalist class. I'm not sure that we know
yet how to face that power with our power for that's not yet
fully realised. The fight for survival, a new phase in the fight
against oppression under late capitalism, may provide that
opportunity, if it is not too late. As writers perhaps all we can
attempt to do is to fight and refight this struggle in language,
to reach out to the furthest limit of the murdering geo-
political abstractions of Reaganism or Thatcherism and

imaginatively help to create the conditions for their refusal, by calling upon our deepest and most passionate desire for life, and by celebrating and recreating our strength.

I don't know. I can only guess. And make myself open. But my thoughts on gender and writing in late summer 1982 are enmeshed in my thoughts on being a woman in this society at this time, on survival and the woman writer's part in that struggle to survive. Any other perspective right now seems academic, in the pejorative sense. Without my life I shall not think or write. As long as I write I must fight, for the life of all I love.

Chapter 6

ON BEING A WOMAN POET

Libby Houston

I begin with the tablecloth: a red brick estate at the north end
of the Piccadilly Line, Oakwood, where c.1949 my first book,
Little Verses by Libby Houston appeared – in print; I hadn't by
then learned to write cursive. Wholehearted plagiarism it
mostly was, of the Flower Fairies, my older brother, anything
– which of course I denied. My headmaster, Haydn Perry, and
Marjorie Kirtley, my teacher, both published children's
poets, encouraged me with glee (I had a poem about imagin-
ary rats read on BBC Children's Hour), but I had no vision of
Being a Poet. Nor any idea of being a woman. I wanted to
explore the Mato Grosso, the veld; my best friend, to be a
sailor. My father, bomber navigator, had been lost in the war.
I was supposed to have his eyes. I was the fattest girl in the
school.

My brother had been away at school since he was seven.
From the eleven-plus I won a bursary to Westonbirt, a refined
and devoutly Protestant girls' boarding school in the
Cotswolds. We were lucky the first year in having to learn a
poem by heart every week. I wrote a sonnet ('. . .Thou dog, art
thou that bright sphere's watchful guard? . . .') to win a book
token (bought Keats) and probably then the expectations of
the English mistress. My mother moved to Clevedon, ex-
watering place on the Bristol Channel.

I think no one could match my compositions for adjectives. In poetry I secretly became as good at loneliness and
death as any teenager – I was good at everything bar games.
After O Level it was *King Lear*, (Mr) Eliot, Radio Luxem-
bourg. We parodied ourselves in fin-de-siècle aesthetic poses,
gazed at the gardener's boy, and I, now attenuated, gave my
first solo public performance imitating Elvis – yes! olive oil in

the hair and eyeshadow under the lower lip (though in fact singing Marvin crack-voiced Rainwater's *Whole Lotta Woman*). I was being groomed to read English at Oxford. By seventeen I was thoroughly institutionalised; I kept my contrary dreams to myself. I have a calligraphic scrap of paper dated 3.12.58 which states: 'Elizabeth Houston doth hereby pronounce her intention to leave her mark upon the world, whether by painting or by writing, by singing or by physical feat.'

I had no preconceptions about Oxford, none whatsoever. The work that became a treadmill of essay-deadlines required analytical argument and thought; my atmospheric descriptions, my photographic memory, counted for little. But it was the constant presence of 'men' that had me reeling, men—who touched me, said they loved me! (Fifteen years later in Kashmir I was just as bewildered, finding that a landscape I had imagined long before and kept as a private reference did actually exist – and thereby redefined me: outsider.) The man (eighteen) who seemed most to embody everything I had ever wanted to be like invited me to – a poetry reading! We hitched – only lorries (he'd already published an anti-academic poem in praise of lorry-drivers, 'England's heroes') – to the Partisan café, Soho, where I saw and heard Mike Horovitz, Pete Brown and others, men, actually standing among a loud and laughing audience reading with wild gestures their own words, and their words, jokes, puns, obscenities! My best friend, a good dressmaker, took in my jeans so tight they needed ankle zips and ruined my veins. I was in love, unspeakably. I stole his poems from the bin. I copied his e's. Reader, as you may imagine, he backed away as nimbly as possible, leaving me with motive and material, O soul of Maud Gonne, to set me on my way like a tank engine on a downhill run.

August, first summer vac (holiday), found me a Beatnik On the Road to the Edinburgh Festival with Pete Brown; among the five of us who dossed down in somebody's kitchen was Mal Dean, working-class art-school drop-out, cartoonist and sick wit from Widnes, whom five years later I married. . . . But then – we were all poets, it was the infection, Live New Departures, cellar readings every night;

without a ticket licence we passed round a hat which just about provided one haggis and chips each a day. Everybody read, their own poems, the Beat heroes', and wrote – pens scratched as you were reading – 'I've got 32 haiku I wrote last night!' (Alan Jackson). Adrian Mitchell, Edwin Morgan, Jerome Rothenberg, Louis Lehmann from Holland raised the tone, musicians, bus-conductors, plain clothes detectives, Icelandic cyclists changed the air, names like Liverpool and Newcastle mingling with Black Mountain, San Francisco, turned magic. There was no criticism, we read our way through gems and rubbish like earth heavers.

When I left Oxford, went down, and received a s.a. postcard rubber-stamped 'CLASS 2' (in green), the prologue ends. Nobody told me what to do next. All this, believe me, is relevant.

We sank like sediment to London, who met in Edinburgh, and lived there, cut off from our roots whether uneducated working-class or genteel, in a heap that sustained and simultaneously hobbled us, Pete Brown, Londoner, at the centre. Being acceptable company, the company, praise, the inspiration we sparked off in each other like the front-line jazz musicians who swapped choruses on the same platforms, kept me writing and giving readings. I'm glad of that apprenticeship: before happenings happened, acid, light shows, electronic blasting and performance art, words on tatty paper were the props, the patter harked back to the Music not the Lecture Hall – and we did entertain.

In that immediate scene I was the only woman I met reading – was it just because I was living in the thick of it? – though there were some in e.g. Liverpool or others published in *New Departures* up-market of myself. But I always identified with the boys. I could flash a smile, dress up, being a woman, part of the act which belonged there. When Horovitz and Brown set about starting a reading agency, *Poetry in Motion*, forerunner of the London and National Poetry Secretariats, eyebrows were raised at me, the woman (apart from Stevie Smith, outside the heap), to run it. I felt the unfairness of the assumption but simply refused in the certainty of being incapable.

Mal and I, being together, gave each other certain

disadvantages: I ruined his chances of beds, meals and drinks at the hands of 'rich women', fans (did my best as a typist, £7 pw starting, two years of it, *Woman's Own*, but it wasn't the same, and I expected hardworking art in return, not tousled breakfasts at my suppertime); would there have been an equivalent rich man at all if I'd been less faithful? We were wretchedly, stupidly poor. It was far beyond my confidence, conditioning, imagining, to initiate, organise anything myself; I joined in gratefully if I was asked and felt peeved if I wasn't.

We married in 1966, and sometime then I was introduced to Clive Allison who was looking for an 'underground' poet to launch himself with Margaret Busby as publishers of cheap-priced poetry paperbacks. I was – an oddity, a potential personality, a woman; a poet. My first book, *A Stained Glass Raree Show*, came out in 1967.

It begins to be a long time ago. I remember facts as if I'd read them in some ambling novel. I try to remember what I thought about writing then.

Ashamed from my first draught of the Beat scene of my rarified background, I became most deeply ashamed of the idea of poetry I had had, the adjectives, bones, gloom, secrecy, poetical language. It came so *easily* to me to wallow solemnly in wool – the sort of wool you find on a dead sheep down a mineshaft. Beat poetry challenged it on the one hand, Eliot's attacks on William Morris's vagueness, Hugh McDiarmid's preposterous plea for an absolutely precise world language, *In Memoriam James Joyce*, on the other. I took their point, made it my aim in writing to scrutinise the implications of every word I used and in performing to entertain. By which of course I'm not just referring to the jokes, patter, dead-pan parodies. I learned at Oxford to love Anglo-Saxon poetry, the rhythm and sound of it, and perhaps by that I came to a musical idea of poetic structure where syllables might scurry past, for instance, as quavers against the crotchet beat – by that and Laurie Morgan's drumming. It's something that does belong to oral literature of a kind, pace is almost impossible to indicate in print. Tennyson found it a problem; Hopkins's accents look uncomfortable on the page.

While I followed fashionable prejudices as the wind blew,

nothing prejudiced me against the narrative poetry, ballads, I'd learned as a child. I found Sidney's praise of story-telling in the *Defence of Poesie* and put my money on it. Being primarily a performer I felt wary of 'confessional' poetry, found disturbing the thought of doling out in public intimate details about someone who might be dumbly listening with their own version, or worse, absent without redress. Besides, when I wrote about Myself, a rather humourless Poetic voice took over, whose honesty I couldn't trust; or I would antici-pate the poem with idea and pat conclusion ready, and never liked doors neatly closed. I trusted invented unanalysed personae and wordplay to tell truths, and to myself, better than my consciousness.

My ancestry's Celtic (Scottish). I loved Yeats; I found in Scottish poetry of all kinds a passion peculiarly absent south of the Border. I didn't come across Sylvia Plath until Alvarez's *Savage God* was in the paper. In *Ariel* I found herself rather than her poems speaking to me, like a desperate person. Stevie Smith I consciously avoided, being still an ace mimic; I was afraid, having heard her once (and liked her) and reckoning myself on a slightly different road, of catching her style inappropriately too easily.

I thought of myself as a person and a poet; never as a woman poet, seldom as a woman.

In 1967, New Year's Eve, our son was born; our daughter in 1970, soon after which my second book *Plain Clothes* also appeared. Without the books and therefore a name occasion-ally chased I should probably have stopped writing. Well! You can't shrug your shoulders in print either.

Read Dr Spock till you can recite him sideways, but out there on your own as a mother you need all the intuition you can muster. If you had it earmarked for writing, it's still requisitioned, must, maybe for good, do double service. That's one thing. And when a baby cries for food, can you say, 'Not this week, I've got a deadline, sorry'? Those demands are commonplace, they can't be put aside; writing can. That's another. Mal, now in the position of having to be earner, didn't compromise, it had to be art or jazz. It wasn't so much that I bowed before Woman's Role; fatherless, I had never had a close-up picture of divided labour. Rather, from school particularly, I had swallowed the precepts of Christianity to my bones – 'Whosoever shall compel thee to go a mile, go with him twain', etc., etc. Which all seemed fair enough. And I hoped that if I – no, I think, more realistically, I felt I couldn't expect let alone ask anything I wasn't willing to give. Willing becoming the operative word.

The first nappy lost me the freewheeling road, the company. Babysitters? We lived in Inner Urban Deprived Area Holloway, my best friends now women like myself, potentially creative (including the first one, who never did make it to sea), hung about with infants, poor, endlessly poor, ex-tomboys who no longer could identify with blokes who drank the money, didn't come home; but we weren't inclined to active politics, we were tired. And liked the company of men, a man, and the pleasure of irrelevant irreverent conversations, anecdotes, jokes. We didn't realise that our men treated us bad because being artists (of all kinds) they had some sensitivity and couldn't cope with it, and holding out confusedly against compromise tried to drown the sound of women crying for cash. And knowing ourselves the value of support to an artist, we were trying like mad to be good supportive wives – we must have engendered so much guilt.

Mal developed cancer in 1972; early in 1974 he died.

I didn't stop writing for two reasons.

First, Paddy Bechely, producer of the BBC Schools Radio series *Stories and Rhymes* (now *Pictures in Your Mind*), asked me on spec to write eight poems about insect metamorphosis for seven-to-eight-year-olds. It just so happened I was keeping an eye on an elephant hawkmoth chrysalis at the time – but writing for an outlet whose sky was never darkened by the spectres of opinionated critics was a pleasure I'd forgotten, no need to wrestle at source with the eager hordes of words only waiting for a chance to prove themselves. Bless her, she has asked me to contribute programmes ever since.

I name names in gratitude: Emma Tennant, then editing the first issue of *Bananas*, asked me for a poem, hounded me to the deadline. I hadn't written a word for a year, turned up an old bitter fragment and working on it found it beginning to work itself, until it presented me – amazed me – with a vision of forgiveness, even Nirvana; she asked me for another. Rock-climbing without a camera I tried words, which settled into a statement on chance and faith. . . . Carol Burns gave me a deadline for *Matrix*, Alan Brownjohn for the Globe Play-house. . . . Two poems a year, or three.

Required to write, reminded like that to write, I knew I also had to write about Mal's death; being there and finding the experience, well, miraculously sweet, I felt it as an obligation to spread good news about something so generally dreaded; if I was a poet then it had to be a poem, above all 'confessional', else the whole point would have been lost. I had *Lycidas* across my path, all my own arguments to meet; it was hard, two years and more, labour.

It's because my poems since that watershed have been about myself, or, if not directly, I have been pretty well aware of their implications from the start, that to make them, finish them, has become an exhausting battle – not only in tricky metaphysical ground to trap the right words, but to keep my analysing conscious self at arm's length while the poem looks for its own conclusion, when I am too weary to hit true first go. And I've thought, if only I could shut myself away for a week. . . .

Before my children, if they should ever read this, feel a rising tide of guilt for existing at all, let me thank them too.

I sometimes worry that I have more of Candide in me than Che Guevara. Besides making me physically fit enough to take up rockclimbing well past thirty – besides being themselves, for heaven's sake – and giving me, as any parent has, a second chance at growing up, my children brought two gifts unexpectedly to my writing. The more obvious was a reacquaintance with legends, fairytales, fables. I've been able to read astoundingly little since they were born – time and habit; or, since I set out into metaphysical regions (Jung's 'land that is not created'?), I've not yet wished to risk picking up anyone else's perceptions lest they falsify my own; or, my head's been crammed like an old coffee filter by too much real life to take in more but seldom. The short, simply-written stories I read aloud gave me clear images to focus on through fog and clutter like coastwise lights.

The second was a new kind of awareness of language.

The greater part of my conversation after Mal died was with small children. I remember my embarrassment at a university poetry reading being confronted by an intellectual question with a head whose currency included no abstract conceptual terminology at all – I couldn't understand it, let alone answer it. But it was a matter of difference, not absolute inadequacy. Any parent should be grateful for the intellectual challenge of explaining God in terms accessible to a three-year-old. Who else is so constantly bombarded with requirements to examine, re-examine, define, explain? 'What's a black hole?' 'Who's Hitler?' etc. – my children – anyone's are – were as unsparing as Socrates, and the answers had to be concrete. When I sat down to write, which was when I was beginning to tackle Great Questions head on, the same language gave me a sure footing. Take such scorned monosyllabic verbs as get, pick, put, etc. and start juggling with the prepositions, possibilities begin to pour.

They grow older; I hope that gift won't wear out.

Well, it became something of a long sentence of isolation. Poetry readings thinned out; or I'd be reading alone, a different matter. And I was writing of necessity for my own needs of elucidation – with an audience or reader still in mind, but not so conjurable as known persons. Back in Holloway, my friends kept moving on until my nearest relationship was with the streets themselves, a neighbourhood that longed, it seemed to me, for the recognised unity-in-diversity of the theoretically ideal (maybe real) village; if it needed poetry, it wasn't the kind I was capable of writing – besides, the place had something of the feel of a UN rehabilitation camp; I think I only never came across a German. I sat on, fell asleep in, every kind of community committee to hand, hoping such a mute expression of naive solidarity might somehow be better than nothing.

My third book, *At the Mercy*, twenty-three poems, ten years' work, came out in 1981.

The Women Live Month in 1982 brought me to meet the Women's Movement for the first time close to. I find its terminology as foreign to me as that of Structuralism, myself as if running in parallel with it, like I do with the established church; I am still tired, still hold an idea of community in immediate streets (Bristol now), my children still the unknown job in hand. I think of the strangeness of my school again, how it not only gave me enough religious questions for life, but being so dedicatedly academic taught me nothing whatsoever about being a housewife, running a home – I would have made such a good irresponsible man poet!

And what does Being a Poet signify? Having by now left some more or less erasable scratches on the world by painting, writing, etc. etc., what pronouncement might I now scribble defiantly to myself? I've had my nose rubbed, over the years, in every single cheerful judgment, whether on persons or literature, I ever made. And since I continue passing judgments I may as well expect a deathbed nose like leather. From the moment I left Oxford and direction disappeared, I've simply been confronting the question of how to live – not (yet), perhaps unfortunately, how to make money to live on, but, under (unforeseen) circumstances, how should a person act?

And in this roughly-plotted territory where snatches of ethics, morals and metaphysics mingle like cloud-shadows, bringing up children and writing poetry interchangeably provide exercises in trying out answers. Out of my unformulated working hypotheses (yes, you can tell, my children are no longer the little pestering kiddies who only ate concrete), the clamour of a deadline will give me the chance of, force me reluctantly into, nailing a perception via poetry. So that it is more than a vehicle of thought; it has become a means of thinking, a route towards understanding. Which I offer to the general pool of literature I use myself; and as I find the work of other writers, odd lines, phrases even, turn up from forgotten corners of my head to illuminate a situation of my own, I'd be glad if mine were able to do the same for other people.

Isolation plays tricks with one's sense of proportion. I clear the table, wash half the plates, notice it's late again, wonder what on earth to cook tomorrow.

Chapter 7

SPEAKING/WRITING/ FEMINISM

Cora Kaplan

My mother describes me at eleven months, a particularly small baby, bundled, propped and harnessed in my pram outside our New York apartment house, addressing startled passers-by with the adult precision of newly learnt speech: 'Hellow, pretty lady!' Speaking came early, came easy, eliciting surprise, approval and even tangible reward. This first gratifying experience of public speaking (I cannot remember it) seemed to set a pattern which allowed me the courage forever after to break through the patriarchal convention that enjoined women to deferential silence. I have always enjoyed the sound of my own voice, even when it has irritated and offended others. As a young political woman my lack of inhibition about public speaking frequently got me into trouble with the male-dominated left. It also, occasionally, got me where I not so secretly wanted to be – on a soapbox, addressing a crowd. In school, at university, but most of all as an academic, this 'unnatural' articulacy has helped to mark me out as a rebel. In professional gatherings where women are in a very small minority, it is normal for them to accept their marginality by staying relatively quiet. My frequent interventions ensure that my social behaviour as well as my opinions are displeasing to my colleagues. In the last fourteen years a very large part of my political and intellectual life has taken place inside the Women's Movement. Of all the changes that feminism has made in my private and public behaviour none has been so hard to learn or to keep to as shutting up so that others may speak.

All forms of public performance seemed to come from a desire that I could neither rationalise or suppress and that overrode self-consciousness. By the time I was nine I had found a relatively acceptable outlet in acting. From then until my early twenties I had no other ambition, and while acting in no way contained my appetite for oral expression, it helped to explain it in terms of an artistic aspiration which could only spring from an eccentric expressive temperament. Nevertheless speaking up, at home, at school, on the stage, always seemed to involve a sense of danger and challenge which I fed on. Writing, on the other hand, was to begin with an act of conformity with family and school. Writing in my Jewish, middle-class intellectual family was the most approved activity. Books and the written word were so highly valued (I was allowed to throw almost anything in a tantrum *except* a book) that my own written efforts were usually accompanied by a kind of terror that they would be derivative, cliché, inauthentic. From my first attempt at fiction, a garbled pastiche of *Lamb's Tales from Shakespeare* called 'The Lovers', to this piece in process, all my narrative or reflexive writing, including letters and diaries, has felt haunted by the language of others. Every fragment of imaginative prose or verse from the age of six onwards has given me that stale ghosted feeling *as I wrote it*, as well as when I read it back afterwards. It took me a long time to find a voice and a genre of writing that gave me the sense that I was cutting across the 'givenness' of social relations.

The difference in my experience of oral and written expression seems worth pursuing for a bit longer, since the causes and effects of the social sanction against women's speech and writing has, for some years now, been the central feminist issue that shapes all my research. Inside my family, as I have said, all the unspoken pressures and desires on and for me, as a precociously clever child, were towards channelling my talents into some sort of writing. To write was to do what my father did and what my mother valued. Talking, or more accurately, talking back, got me into endless trouble. My childhood and adolescence was one long struggle with a paternal authority which had imagined a gentler, more docile daughter. Neither of my parents thought much of my dramatic ambitions or talents though they did nothing to discourage me; on the contrary they made considerable sacrifices of time and money to help me along. Yet I could not fail to understand their disappointment. A sort of political puritanism made the exploitation of one's own voice and body too bound up with egotism and personal desires. In writing, the family morality seemed to say, the suspect personal gratifications of self-expression were reduced to an acceptable, ethical level through the displacement of words from mouth to printed page. This implicit critique of theatrical self-presentation became linked for me with the whole range of frivolous, sensual, self-indulgent activities from dressing up – an elaborate event in the 1950s – to secret masturbation. All these were practices my parents disapproved of, or would have done, I was sure, if they had known about them. Acting, speaking, showing off my adolescent body, worst of all touching it, were, I was convinced, tainted in my parents' eyes with egotism in general and female narcissism in particular. Dressing up and showing off were complicit in their minds with the worst aspects of femininity as the dominant culture decreed it. How much of this was projected guilt is hard to tell. I couldn't have put all these impressions into words in my teens. Still, if anyone had asked me what their model of a good socialist woman was I would have been able to describe her. She was the woman who had ignored her emergent sexuality in adolescence, sublimated desire, dressed and spoke soberly and used the last leisured years of childhood to learn that she might teach. I was a child of the 1950s and Rosa Luxemburg was a remote and scary figure. My heroine, in so far as I had one, was Sarah Bernhardt. As Hamlet.

The 1950s for left-wing Americans were a frightening, demoralising decade. Our family clung together. I kept secrets that I had never been told. I shared my parents' politics – (how could I not? – I still do in great part) and found it difficult to criticise the social inflections of their views. In some upside-down way writing became saturated with a set of ethical prescriptions that I could neither refuse nor wholly accept. It became what others desired of me, and only sometimes what I wanted for and of myself. It became the other of an illicit, politically incorrect femininity in which I desperately wanted to be inscribed, the other too, of my formidable and undervalued ambitions as an actress. Although I gave voice to the words of the playwright on the local stage it was there, above all, that I felt I uttered myself. For a very long time, longer than I care to think, even *now*, writing is too often the act of a dutiful daughter. It was at my desk and my typewriter that I felt spoken, not by the culture that disapproved of women writing only a little less than it disliked women speaking in public, but by that powerful alternative culture in which I was raised.

In my personal history, then, the psychic contradiction between woman's speech and her femininity was given an eccentric twist. If the construction of femininity roughly follows the dominant psychic structures of a given society, any particular instance will have its own inflection. While I understand, as an abstraction, that my wilfully raised voice usurps 'the place and tone of a man', for me speaking out is also deeply entwined with femininity, with, for example, a conventional desire to be looked at. That extended angry verbal struggle with my father – what did I have but words to get his attention, to intervene between him and my mother, and what did he give me back but words? For many women sexuality is spoken through their social silence. For me, language did what my meagre child's body (I could pass easily for ten or eleven at seventeen) could never do. In recent years I have been giving more and more public lectures, often to audiences of women only, but invariably on feminist subjects. My talks are never given from a written text; I rarely refer to notes. These occasions bring the ethical and political imperatives through which I was raised together with my irrepressible and unregenerate desire to speak out, to have a direct, unmediated contact with an audience. Very often the subject of these talks mirrors the meaning of the event for me – an historical and theoretical account of the related suppression of women's speech, writing and sexuality.

There still remains the difficult subject of this essay – my own writing. I have deferred it as long as I could, deferred the actual writing of this section for months because I thought that I could not bear to see what I would say. As I get older – I am forty-two as I write this – the possibility of writing has largely replaced the possibility of new emotional and sexual adventures as a subject for fantasy. It is the activity in which I would now prefer to recognise myself. 'Writer' ranks way above 'mother', 'teacher', 'speaker', as a vocational identity. As a young woman, writing seemed to threaten femininity – to leave me stranded on the dry shores of the incest taboo, my father's daughter and no one's lover. Now, when I feel sure that no one will love me in the body who does not first love me for my words, writing promises too much in the way of fantasised libidinal reward instead of too little. There seems often to be too much invested in its success: political effectiveness, professional status, recognition within feminism, the self-respect that comes with completing a self-imposed task, and sometimes pleasure in the process itself. How did this puritanical work, so often in my teens and twenties an escape from the insistent desire of and for a man, become, in my thirties, the process and polemic of desire? What follows is a narrative that has been only partly worked through. I do not see it as typical or representative. I offer it with some diffidence as a history which might contribute something to the understanding of the relationship of women to writing.

In 1973 I was separated from my husband with a five-year-old child to support, a university job that I needed to hold on to and an ugly battle to acquire academic tenure ahead. I was thirty-three years old and had been working on an unfinished DPhil thesis for some seven years. The subject – Tom Paine and the radical press in the late eighteenth century – was partly inherited from my father who as a young man had adopted Paine as one of his radical heroes. I too was drawn to Paine for his marvellous popular rhetoric, his democratic politics, his personal eccentricities and his vision of self-determination based on a dream of universal literacy. Paine was a figure easily appropriated to the new left politics in which I had been involved in America. Perhaps he was a bit too like the young male left who wanted the women in the movement as tea-makers, typists, envelope lickers, and, in the memorable words of Stokely Carmichael – 'prone'. Certainly the topic was top-heavy with associations that made me nervous of it as well as fascinated by it. In any case I was working on this thesis at some disadvantage, 3,000 miles away from not one but three supervisors, a benign but internally divided trinity of male historians. By 1973 the subject had gone a bit stale on me and I had outgrown the liberal paradigm in which the original project was couched without having acquired the theoretical tools to reformulate it. I had made myself politically extremely unpopular at my workplace by taking an active and vocal part in a bitter row about free speech and the Vietnam War, which split my department and made my subject chairman into an enemy. Even so, he thought well of the thesis, and it seemed crucial that I complete it in order to be given tenure.

At this point, with everything pressing me towards doing what was asked of me by my institution, I abandoned the dissertation, not formally but quite definitively, and began an entirely different project – the construction of a critical anthology of women's poetry. I found a publisher, negotiated a fee and finished the book in about eighteen months. It, and not my uncompleted work on Paine, was assessed finally as the research which secured my job. I have never touched the thesis again, nor have I ever written to my supervisors to explain why. I knew that it was impossible for me to write anything more for the judgment of those fair-minded, affectionate men, nor could I find a language adequate to explain my defection as something other than disability.

Perhaps I should have sent them a copy of the anthology, for in the introductory essay I described women's embattled relationship to poetry, the most highly valued discourse in western culture. There, too, I spoke of the ways in which writing poetry involved women in complex moments that were simultaneously resistant and submissive to the dominant patriarchal culture. There were analogies to my own history, but I did not try to think about them. I never sent my supervisors either the book or a letter of explanation; my boorish silence must have satisfied some need in me for a violent and irrevocable break with a project too intimately tied up with my family. For when I abandoned the dissertation I also seem to have stopped writing simply through and for my father's desire. My thesis especially, but much of the writing I had done as undergraduate and postgraduate were, I now think, intended above all to win my father's approval.

Metaphorically these pieces had use value only; I made them for domestic consumption. In so far as they served to further my career as an academic that career too became bound to my father's will, in ways that made me, in the first years as a teacher, dislike this 'second choice' profession as if it were a forced marriage.

At that particular moment in my life, the marketplace offered and supported a kind of freedom, capitalist in its terms, that I could not find in the academy. Because of my personal history, writing for the university system became writing for patriarchy par excellence. It was extraordinarily important to me that my anthology was paid for, circulated and sold, for at that time feminism had almost no purchase or currency within English universities, and especially not within literary studies. In evading some of the conditions of production imposed by the institution and in redefining my subject I had, at last, found a place from which I could write, as I could speak, to a wider audience than one man.

The 'self' that occupies the place-from-which-I-can – write exists as a necessary fiction for writing, a sometimes fantasy of autonomy and authority that persists, if I am exceptionally lucky, until the end of the writing project. There is a temptation, which has found its way into much recent feminist criticism, to celebrate this writing identity both as a temporary escape from femininity, and as a model for a post-feminist female identity which will endure through the history of an individual. It is perhaps a common-sense indulgence to see woman in this supposed moment of defiance and rupture as woman as she must become outside and beyond patriarchal inscription. While I think that defiance is a component of the act of writing for women, I would now prefer to emphasise the fluctuant nature of subjectivity which the contrast between the writing and non-writing identity highlights.

In the early stages of thinking about women and writing I had, in common with other feminists, talked mostly about the ways in which women were denied access to something I have called 'full' subjectivity. While any term so abstract evokes more meaning than it can possibly contain in a given context, what I was working towards was a description of a position within culture where women could, without impediment, exist as speaking subjects. I now think that this way of posing the question of writing/speaking and subjectivity is misleading. It assumes, for instance, that *men* write from a realised and realisable autonomy in which they are, in fact, not fantasy, the conscious, constant and triumphant sources of the meanings they produce. This assumption is part of an unreconstructed romantic definition of the poet as it was most eloquently expressed in Wordsworth's 1800 introduction to *Lyrical Ballads*. Here the poet has a universalised access to experience of all kinds, feels things more deeply, and expresses those feelings 'recollected in tranquillity' for all men. It did not take much thought to point out how difficult it was for women to appropriate this romantic definition of genius and transcendence, given the contemporary restraints on their experience and the contempt in which their gender-specific feelings were held. A more interesting question was about the status of the definition itself which even today has enormous currency within traditional literary criticism. How far was it an ideological fiction? In what sense could any writing or writer – widen the thing defined, the romantics did – any *actor* in history *be* that romantic subject? For if one were to accept a modern reworking of the romantic definition of the creative process, then as a feminist 'full subjectivity' would become a political goal for feminism, as well as a precondition for all acts of struggle and intervention, writing included.

In the last few years I have come round to a very different perspective on the problem, drawn from Marxist and feminist appropriations of psychoanalytic and structuralist theories, but confirmed, I think, by my own and other women's fragmented experience of writing and identity. Rather than approach women's difficulty in positioning themselves as writers as a question of barred access to some durable psychic state to which all humans should and can aspire, we might instead see their experience as foregrounding the inherently unstable and split character of all human subjectivity. Within contemporary western culture the act of writing and the romantic ideologies of individual agency and power are tightly bound together, although that which is written frequently resists and exposes this unity of the self as ideology. At both the psychic and social level, always intertwined, women's subordinate place within culture makes them less able to embrace or be held by romantic individualism with all its pleasures and dangers. The instability of 'femininity' as female identity is a specific instability, an eccentric relation to the construction of sexual difference, but it also points to the fractured and fluctuant condition of all consciously held identity, the impossibility of a will-full, unified and cohered subject.

Romantic ideologies of the subject suppress this crucial and potentially hopeful incoherence, or make its absence a sign of weakness and thus an occasion for mourning or reparation. Feminism has been caught up far too often in this elegaic mood, even when on other fronts it has mounted an impressive critique of Western rationalism as a phallocratic discourse of power. One option within feminism to combat the seeming weakness which inheres in women's split subjectivity has been to reassert an economy of control, to deny the constant effect of unconscious processes in utterance and practice, and to pose an unproblematic rationalism for women themselves, a feminist psyche in control of femininity. For myself, this avenue is closed, if only because it makes me feel so demoralised, a not-good-enough feminist as I was a not-good-enough daughter. I would rather see subjectivity as always in process and contradiction, even female subjectivity, structured, divided and denigrated through the matrices of sexual difference. I see this understanding as part of a more optimistic political scenario than the ones I have been part of, one that can and ought to lead to a politics which will no longer overvalue control, rationality and individual power, and which, instead, tries to understand human desire, struggle and agency as they are mobilised through a more complicated, less finished and less heroic psychic schema.

This perspective makes better sense of my own experience as writer and speaker, both as a dutiful daughter and now as a feminist, and gives me some clues as to what enabled the passage between these two moments. Neither activity or position has given me a security of identity nor do I any longer see that as a meaningful objective. However, the stake

and contradictions involved in writing and speaking as a
feminist have shifted, although not always in easily apparent
ways. The way I write has hardly changed since I was an
undergraduate. I always favoured a rich, fruity prose,
leavened and larded with word play and jokes which fleshed
out the didactic skeleton of my arguments and broke up the
high seriousness of academic discourse. Puns and risqué
metaphors are a way of making the hard puritanical business
of writing more fun, more libidinal, and therefore, more
mine. I never need to tell jokes when I am giving a talk, nor do
they seem to be necessary to hold an audience to a serious
theme. Speaking involves a bodily presence, is itself a
pleasure. However, in the teaching situation, in the solemn,
tense occasion of tutorial or seminar, vulgar wise-cracks
spring to my lips unbidden. I understand better now, why I
make these formal rhetorical choices. That knowledge in
itself has changed the condition of utterance.

Tillie Olsen, the American writer and critic, has
explored the multiple ways in which women's silences as
writers have been overdetermined in western culture. Her
overview is always both Marxist and feminist, but she always
emphasises the importance of the individual situation. In my
own family history the dominant prejudices against female
utterance were only ever mobilised against my speaking
voice. It is that voice from a position of opposition that has
emerged confident, playful and fluent. My pleasure and confidence in writing has been as hard to achieve as unreliable,
though at certain rare moments as thrilling as sexual
pleasure. Familial disavowal and/or support always has
complex and mediated effects in relation to dominant
ideologies. All my published writing has been within and for
feminism. These days, however, the conditions of production
have shifted. Now I write into a constituted discipline of
recognised intellectual importance. I write for women, rather
than as in my early work, constructing a polemic directed
against men. And I have noticed a change in the content and
direction of my work which is a bit worrying. The critical
sections of the poetry anthology were almost always positive
appraisals, a revision and revaluation of lost or dismissed
writing. These days I have moved away from mildly

eulogistic projects, and instead have engaged in a series of fairly heavy debates with other feminists and other feminisms, historical and contemporary. This internal polemic suggests that the habit of writing in opposition is deeply ingrained, in fact the only tolerable mode of writing for me. Even within the women's movement which has given purpose and meaning to my life and my words, I remain something of an ungrateful child.

Chapter 8

QUESTIONS AND ANSWERS

Michele Roberts

I didn't want to write these notes at all when Michelene first asked me to do so. I felt, somewhat tetchily, that the discussion of my relationship to gender and to writing is contained, often quite explicitly, in my poems and novels. In fact, I think, I wanted to stun the world with a dazzling piece of literary theory and knew I wouldn't be able to do it. Michelene patiently repeated that what she wanted was a personal, not a theoretical account.

What finally determined me to write this piece was an experience I had two weeks ago. I'd been asked to give a reading of my poetry by a small local poetry group in southwest London. I chose poems that I thought illustrated my interest in the feminine as powerful, angry, passionate, sexual, creative. I read poems about Amazons, sibyls, mother goddesses; poems criticising male sadism, desires for omnipotence, scorn of women; poems mourning my loss of my mother, my grandmother. When I'd finished reading, the audience, mainly male, responded. 'If you're a feminist, why don't you write more aggressively?' one man asked: 'why don't you smash the world up, smash things apart?' Another man said: 'Feminism's a load of crap, it went out with the sixties.' And another man said: 'The thing I like about your poems is they're so *androgynous* – you don't speak as a woman at all.' After a passionate discussion, in which the one woman in the audience managed to make herself heard through the men's constant interruptions and said she found my poems moving and stimulating, I went home feeling angry. Discussion with a woman friend (Sian Dodderidge – to whom many thanks) provoked the following reflections. Men often can't hear women speaking *as women*: they can only hear anger, for example, expressed in masculine terms: aggro, smashing things up. My poems invite an audience to listen, to open up, to take images inside. Clearly this is threatening to some men, since it suggests a feminine activity: embracing, holding; a power they're frightened of. The men that night seemed to be saying: all we can understand is beating up or being beaten up. I had no desire to be big momma with a stick (in my poetic discourse) smacking them for naughtiness; yet they seemed *incapable* of entering into an equal relationship with my poems and language.

So here it is. It's not coherent as a whole, because my thoughts about my writing are always in flux. It's a report on progress and process as I see it at the time of writing (October 1982), written in fragments which may or may not connect with each other.

Who is the writer?

In one sense it's very simple. I'm female: I use female images to describe the various processes involved in creating a poem or novel. The nun contemplates in silence. The housewife creates order out of chaos. The sibyl is possessed by the goddess. The priestess declaims to the listening people. The mother conceives an idea. The midwife aids the birth.

These images feel natural to me now, but didn't always. I had to find them; I struggled to find them. I needed to name myself in a way that connected female-powerful-creator. Opening up to the mythic constellations of the unconscious enabled me to begin to write, indicated to me what I needed to write about, suggested attitudes towards the writing process itself.

One day it will be obvious that there are male writers and female writers, rather than, as at present, female writers and writers (read *real, male*). We're not there yet. We've got to continue through the process, initiated by women, of recognising masculine and feminine experience, aspects of the psyche. Men have got to come out as *men*. This will alter their prose.

Why do I write?

Accepting and questioning my femaleness is inseparable

from accepting and questioning my drive to write. I have always wanted to be a writer, and have written since early childhood. In adolescence, increasing alienation from myself and from the view of femininity purveyed by the late 1950s/ early 1960s culture drove me and my writing underground; I stopped being honest with myself and others about what I felt, and tried to please, and kept my poems, my authentic records, secret. I came out as a poet when I found the Women's Liberation Movement in 1970 and realised that I wasn't mad so much as confused and angry.

When I began trying to analyse (because I was asked to) my need to write, several years ago, I came up with an explanation I tracked down as echoing aspects of the work of Sigmund Freud and Melanie Klein. I know that I write out of the experience of loss; the earliest experience of that is the loss of my mother. Loss is an emptiness filled with terrifying feelings: burning hate, sizzling despair, rage that tears you apart. I hated my mother (the fantasy image of her I constructed inside myself) for not always being there when I wanted her, or as much as I needed. She hadn't wanted twin daughters, but a son. Hate sets up in turn the need for love, to move back into love; hate impelled me to fill up its emptiness with images I could take back to my mother (in my imagination) and offer her as gifts, emblems of my need for her forgiveness, for her love. In real life this was difficult; my mother found my writing an attack on her, since I wrote about sexuality and daughters' difficult relationships with our mothers, and criticised the Catholic faith in which she'd brought me up. Recently, I've found that this need to make reparation, to repair losses, has been characterised more by grief than by rage, and I'm clearer that it happens inside me, and that I need to forgive myself as much as ask my mother to do so. Over the years she and I *have* forgiven each other. She worries about me less since I have become more established as a writer, delights me by reading and criticising what I write, gets all her friends to buy my books. I recognise how like her I am in many ways, an identification not possible for a long time. We differ too, and that seems to feel all right now for both of us. Recently I wrote a poem explicitly dedicated to her (the first really affirmatory one) in which I named her as

Demeter, the harvest goddess who keeps going, doing all the necessary tasks of collecting, sorting, storing, compost-making, and who therefore makes it possible for the seasons to turn, for the new shoots to grow in the spring, for the buried daughter Persephone to rise. This poem is an acknowledgment of dependency and love I haven't been able to make before.

So if I'm no longer writing out of such strong hate and grief around loss, what am I writing from? I now see the loss as on a different, larger scale, and the reparation likewise. I still think that women, though embedded in the heart, factory and kitchen of culture, are treated as though we are peripheral to it; and many of us feel like exiles. Certainly my new (unfinished) novel tackles the theme of separation on this scale. I'm now writing about the mother principle, the feminine principle (as distinct from my own personal mother); certainly these are repressed in a patriarchal culture.

Another definition of writing has to do with play: something I thought women had to give up at puberty in exchange for dedication to the needs of others. Play: making a mess, moulding mud into pies and sculptures, tearing up bits of paper and reassembling them in patterns, mixing water paints and splashing them around, digging for treasures, fishing, exploring unknown places, finding out how things work, exploring the bodies of other children. I enjoy writing tremendously (though it terrifies me too and often I'm exploring the unknown); the pleasure of playing alone (writing) caused me guilt for years and reminded me of adolescent Catholic guilt about masturbation. It's interesting how often the terms self-indulgent and wanky are applied to personal or confessional writing. . . .

Where do I write?
I live alone. The cupboard-kitchen opens off the big bed-sitting-room. I like writing at the table which also serves as washing-up rack, chopping board, eating place, and I like being near the coffee and the food. I write in bed quite often too, and that reminds me of the sibyl's cave: duvet drawn up over the head and I enter another world from this one we call

'real'. My room reminds me, contentedly, of my unconscious: chaotic, in need of a sorting-out. I'd like (I think) to live with another person and have a child; but I'd be desperate and impossible to live with if I didn't have a room of my own in which to spread out and feel comfortable. I shared a room with my two sisters until I left home at eighteen; I made myself a doll's room in my bedside table cupboard, which was curved, and body-shaped. Inside it lived my doll, busy writing.

How do I write?

You can't separate form from content. But I will. I'm influenced by the rituals and forms of worship of the Catholic church, by their language and rhythms. The Office which divides the day into moments of particular prayer; the liturgy which divides the year into seasons of growth, death, birth; the Mass which celebrates union and community in a complex symphony of prayers and psalms; the sacraments; the litany of praise to the Virgin. These rhythms of language, and particularly those of the psalms, are inside me now like my bones. I took them in like my mother's milk: a French Roman Catholic, my mother spoke French to us and brought us up bilingual. I'm also influenced by the rhythms of my English grandmother's voice, as she babysat for us children and made up rude rhyming epics, by the sound of the Chaucer and Shakespeare I studied at university.

Recently, I read somewhere a definition of modernism which suggested that it starts with fragmentation of the authorial self (the splits and zigzags also recorded by Freud and Einstein) and progresses towards the intention to renew tradition by reaffirming an underlying order in history accessible at the level of myth. This interests me when I try to think about my own writing, since for a long time I have been preoccupied with the fragmentation and splits I feel, and record as a novelist and poet, and which I associate with the psychic dismemberment of the female in this culture: whore/ madonna, you've got a body *or* a soul, you've got brains *or* beauty, you can't be a mother *and* an artist, etc.

I find it hard to write about anything that is a whole or is a beautiful simple unity, and yet that is what the novels and poems I grew up on implied was possible. I've had to see things as broken, separated into their component parts, and these I am examining, through the process of metaphor. Thus the narratives I employ cannot possibly be single lines in time, from A to Z: I have to go backwards and forwards and around, just as the eye travels in a cubist painting. Narrative turns into glue; I'm an archaeologist reassembling shards of pottery I've found. It's important that you see the lines of glue so that you realise that I made up the pot; it's not the original (how can I know what that looked like?) but my own version, my own myth.

Yet I yearn for unity, yearn to repair the pot, to make reparation. So I've turned more and more to the unconscious, to the ancient memories therein, to resurrect mythic (this does not mean *false*, but *created*) constellations of aspects of the self and others. I've been encouraged by Jungian feminist/women writers who have named a four-fold constellation of the female psyche: mother (creating babies and art); lesbian (lover of women who may also be mother); companion to men (lover, comrade); sibyl (woman who gives birth to poetry and art). These archetypes are said to exist in every woman. I was surprised to find that I wrote poems on these aspects of woman *before* I read about them in books. So, yes, I end up, after the exploration of splitting, breaking, fragmenting, to some extent writing holistically. I worry that this is bad, incorrect, romantic. But new conflicts always surface and demand to be written about. As soon as I complete one myth, another conflict erupts and demands to be dealt with.

What do I write about?
I write about conflicts. Questions arise urgently, and demand answers. My first novel asked and tried to answer the question: how can women love each other; and I used the icons of the nun and the lesbian, both being women without men. My second novel asked and tried to answer the question: can a woman create art with a gendered voice; and I used the figure of the male-female twins, the problem of masculine-feminine, heterosexuality versus female friendship. My third novel is asking the question: what is the relationship of the body to the soul; and is using the images of the prostitute, the

abandoned child, the man confronting his longing for the mother.

The word *mystical* carries pejorative connotations for many people. Yet it's crucial for a writer to examine what we call reality, and to explore the relationship of language to different sorts of reality. The reality we perceive via the senses and the intellect is only one. There is another: the experience of a co-existing world/landscape where past and future dance in an eternal present. I can *call* this 'the unconscious'; 'the feminine'; 'God'; 'the irrational'; or I can *explore* it through writing poetry and novels. This world I imagine through darkness. Ways in can be through dreams, sleeping or waking. The bed as sibylline cave. The body, my female body, is that cave. The body is the way in to that other world. We do not have to transcend the body in order to find it. The live body works and sleeps and loves above ground. The dead body decays below ground and enriches the earth. We're all part of the nitrogen cycle, the dance of atoms. Life begins below ground; the plants push up their green tips after the long death of winter. The repressed feminine principle struggles for birth. The female body, my knowledge of it, becomes part of my prose questioning whether we simply move in cycles, death leading to rebirth, birth leading to growth leading to death leading to rebirth, in an eternal cycle, or whether our hard-gained feminist knowledge can push onwards our consciousness (from a fuller knowledge of our unconscious) towards *change*. I'm back to Demeter and Persephone: what does Persephone's sojourn underground teach her, and what does she tell Demeter on her return?

Chapter 9

NOTES FROM THE FRONT LINE

Angela Carter

I've just scrapped my sixth attempt to write something for this book because my ideas get quite out of hand the minute I try to put them down on paper and I flush hares out of my brain which I then pursue, to the detriment of rational discourse. To try to say something simple – do I 'situate myself politically as a writer'? Well, yes; of course. I always hope it's obvious, although I try, when I write fiction, to think on my feet – to present a number of propositions in a variety of different ways, and to leave the reader to construct her own fiction for herself from the elements of my fictions. (Reading is just as creative an activity as writing and most intellectual development depends upon new readings of old texts. I am all for putting new wine in old bottles, especially if the pressure of the new wine makes the old bottles explode.)

The Women's Movement has been of immense importance to me personally and I would regard myself as a feminist writer, because I'm a feminist in everything else and one can't compartmentalise these things in one's life. My work *has* changed a good deal in the last ten or fifteen years; it would have been rather shocking if it hadn't, since, during that time, I've progressed from youth to middle age, and, for me, growing into feminism was part of the process of maturing. But when I look at the novels I wrote in my twenties, when I was a girl, I don't see a difference in the emotional content, or even in the basic themes; I recognise myself, asking questions, sometimes finding different answers than I would do now. I also see myself expressing myself in quite different ways now that I'm capable of subjecting to critical analysis problems that, when I was younger and perhaps bruised more easily, I perceived and interpreted in a much more intuitive and also much more self-defensive way. For example, I used the strategy of charm a good deal – I attempted to disarm with charm, in a way that makes me feel affectionately indulgent and maternal to the young person I was, who wanted so much to be loved.

I'm forty-two now; therefore I was a young woman during the 1960s. There is a tendency to underplay, even to completely devalue, the experience of the 1960s, especially for women, but towards the end of that decade there was a brief period of public philosophical awareness that occurs only very occasionally in human history; when, truly, it felt like Year One, that all that was holy was in the process of being profaned and we were attempting to grapple with the real relations between human beings. So writers like Marcuse and Adorno were as much part of my personal process of maturing into feminism as experiments with my sexual and emotional life and with various intellectual adventures in anarcho-surrealism. Furthermore, at a very unpretentious level, we were truly asking ourselves questions about the nature of reality. Most of us may not have come up with very startling answers and some of us scared ourselves good and proper and retreated into cul-de-sacs of infantile mysticism; false prophets, loonies and charlatans freely roamed the streets. But even so, I can date to that time and to some of those debates and to that sense of heightened awareness of the society around me in the summer of 1968, my own questioning of the nature of my reality as a *woman*. How that social fiction of my 'femininity' was created, by means outside my control, and palmed off on me as the real thing.

This investigation of the social fictions that regulate our lives – what Blake called the 'mind-forg'd manacles' – is what I've concerned myself with consciously since that time. (I realise, now, I must always have sensed that something was badly wrong with the versions of reality I was offered that took certain aspects of my being *as* a woman for granted. I smelled the rat in D. H. Lawrence pretty damn quick.) This is also the product of an absolute and committed materialism – i.e., that *this* world is all that there is, and in order to question the nature of reality one must move from a strongly grounded base in what constitutes material reality. Therefore I become mildly irritated (I'm sorry!) when people, as they sometimes do, ask me about the 'mythic quality' of work I've written lately. Because I believe that all myths are products of the human mind and reflect only aspects of material human practice. I'm in the demythologising business.

I'm interested in myths – though I'm much more interested in folklore – just because they *are* extraordinary lies designed to make people unfree. (Whereas, in fact, folklore is a much more straightforward set of devices for making real life more exciting and is much easier to infiltrate with different kinds of consciousness.) I wrote one anti-mythic novel in 1977, *The Passion of New Eve* – I conceived it as a feminist tract about the social creation of femininity, amongst other things – and relaxed into folklore with a book of stories about fairy stories, *The Bloody Chamber*, in 1979. It turned out to be easier to deal with the shifting structures of reality and sexuality by using sets of shifting structures derived from orally transmitted traditional tales. Before that, I used bits and pieces from various mythologies quite casually, because they were to hand.

To return to that confused young person in her early twenties attempting to explicate the world to herself via her craft, the person in the process of becoming radically sceptical, that is, if not free, then more free than I had been. Apart from feeling a treacherous necessity to charm, especially when, however unconsciously, I was going straight for the testicles, I was, as a girl, suffering a degree of colonialisation of the mind. Especially in the journalism I was writing then, I'd – quite unconsciously – posit a male point of view as a general one. So there was an element of the male impersonator about this young person as she was finding herself. For example, in a piece about the suburb of Tokyo I lived in in 1969, I described the place thus: 'It has everything a reasonable man could want . . . massage parlours and, etc.' I used the phrase, 'a reasonable man', quite without irony, although, reading the piece in 1982, it is, ironically, most fitting – the suburb *did* boast all the conveniences a 'reasonable man' might want, although a reasonable woman might have found them inessential, to say the least.

When the piece was republished in a collection of essays

last year, I wondered whether to insert 'sic' in brackets after that 'reasonable man' but then I thought, no; that's cheating. Because my female consciousness *was* being forged out of the contradictions of my experience as a traveller, as, indeed, some other aspects of my political consciousness were being forged. (It was a painful and enlightening experience to be regarded as a coloured person, for example; to be defined as a Caucasian before I was defined as a woman, and learning the hard way that most people on this planet are *not* Caucasian and have no reason to either love or respect Caucasians.)

By the way, I make my living as a writer and have done so most of my adult life. This is no big deal and doesn't mean I always made much money. It has always been easier for me to cut my life-style to suit my income than the other way round so it's always been possible to manage. On the rare occasions when I've attempted to work within a hierarchical framework, when you have to get to an office on time and so on, and be nice to people you don't actually like, much, things have always gone badly. Because I've almost always been self-employed, I've had very little experience, as a woman, of the hurly-burly of mixed-sex working life. I get messages through from the front line that fill me with grief and fury for my sisters out there but this is different from personal experience. For some reason, I've almost always worked with women editors at my various publishing houses, and, even when one is dealing with a woman with zero feminist consciousness, there *is* a difference. Since it was, therefore, primarily through my sexual and emotional life that I was radicalised – that I first became truly aware of the difference between how I was and how I was supposed to be, or expected to be – I found myself, as I grew older, increasingly writing about sexuality and its manifestations in human practice. And I found most of my raw material in the lumber room of the Western European imagination.

Let me explain this. It seems obvious, to an impartial observer, that Western European civilisation as we know it has just about run its course and the emergence of the Women's Movement, and all that implies, is both symptom and product of the unravelling of the culture based on Judaeo-Christianity, a bit of Greek transcendentalism via the father of lies, Plato, and all the other bits and pieces. As a Japanese friend of mine once said, the spotlight of history is moving inexorably away from Europe towards Asia and Africa – societies that we (and white women can't get out of our historic complicity in colonialism, any more than the white working class can) comprehensively screwed, that owe us nothing and expect nothing whatsoever from us, which is just as well as the idea we might actually owe *them* something, like cash, doesn't go down too well, certainly in Britain. It is possible, assuming Western Europe is permitted to sidle out of the spotlight of history rather than going up with a bang, that, for the first time for a thousand years or so, its inhabitants may at last be free of their terrible history.

The sense of limitless freedom that I, as a woman, sometimes feel *is* that of a new kind of being. Because I simply could not have existed, as I am, in any other preceding time or place. I am the pure product of an advanced, industrialised, post-imperialist country in decline. But this has very little to do with my ability to work as I please, or even to earn a living from writing. At any time up to the early twentieth century, I could have told as many stories as I wanted, and made them as wonderful and subversive as I wished, had I survived the births of my children or the hazards of working-class or peasant life to a sufficient age to have amassed a repertoire of orally-transmitted fiction. If I'd been born an aristocrat, I could certainly have become very famous and honoured as an actual writer in medieval Japan, where there were many women writers of fiction and poetry, and where human ingenuity in sexual practice (unrestricted by the Judaeo-Christian ethic, which they knew nothing about) certainly seems to have made sexual intercourse less onerously fruitful than in the West. I could have been a professional writer at any period since the seventeenth century in Britain or in France. But I could *not* have combined this latter with a life as a sexually active woman until the introduction of contraception, unless I had been lucky enough to have been born sterile, as George Eliot must have been. Even if I had been rich enough to afford child care, wealth was no protection against puerperal fever, and being pregnant most of the time is tiring, enfeebling, and a drain on one's physical and emotional resources. In fact, most women were *ill* most of the time until the introduction of contraception and efficient post- and ante-natal care and you need to be quite strong and healthy to write big, fat books. (You do also need to have been around.)

And, just as I write this, I recall a bizarre contradiction. For the past three centuries in Europe, women have excelled – and been honoured for it – in the performing arts. Acting, singing, dancing, playing musical instruments. For some reason, the Women's Movement tends to overlook all that, perhaps because it seems less 'creative' to play somebody else's piano concerto beautifully than it is to write the thing. But it certainly takes a good deal more physical energy to perform a piano concerto than it does to write one, and weak, feeble women have been strumming away, sometimes in the last stages of pregnancy, ever since they were let up on the podium. It *is* odd. Like so many girls, I passionately wanted to be an actress when I was in my early teens and I turn this (balked, unachieved and now totally unregretted) ambition over in my mind from time to time. Why did it seem so pressing, the need to demonstrate in public a total control and transformation of roles other people had conceived? Rum, that.

However. A 'new kind of being', unburdened with a past. The voluntarily sterile yet sexually active being, existing in more than a few numbers, *is* a being without precedent and, by voluntarily sterile, I don't necessarily mean permanently childless; this category includes women who are sterile not all, just most of the time, after all. I/we are not the slaves of the history that enslaved our ancestors, to quote Franz Fanon (although he meant specifically chattel slavery).

So I feel free to loot and rummage in an official past, specifically a literary past, but I like paintings and sculptures and the movies and folklore and heresies, too. This past, for me, has important decorative, ornamental functions; further, it is a vast repository of outmoded lies, where you can check out what lies used to be à la mode and find the old lies on which new lies have been based.

There are one or two lies in the lumber room about the artist, about how terrific it is to be an artist, how you've got to suffer and how artists are wise and good people and a whole lot of crap like that. I'd like to say something about that, because writing – to cite one art – is only applied linguistics and Shelley was wrong, we're *not* the unacknowledged legislators of mankind. Some women really do seem to think they will somehow feel better or be better if they get it down on paper. I don't know.

Writing – the only art form I know too much about, as practice – certainly doesn't make better people, nor do writers lead happier lives. How can I put it; although I might have liked to write poetry like Baudelaire's, I certainly would not, for one single minute, have wanted the kind of life that Baudelaire lived. His poetry is the product of terminal despair, and he was a shit, to boot. It is easy to forget that most of the great male geniuses of Western European culture have been either depraved egomaniacs or people who led the most distressing lives. (My two male literary heroes, Melville and Dostoievsky, were both rather fine human beings, as it turns out, but both of them lived so close to the edge of the existential abyss that they must often, and with good reason, have envied those who did not have enquiring minds.) I'm not saying it's great to be a cow, just keep on chewing the cud, although I have nothing against cows nor, for that matter, against enquiring minds. Only, that posthumous fame is no comfort at all and the actual satisfactions of artistic production are peculiarly lonely and solipsistic ones, while the work itself has the same compensations as those of any self-employed worker, no more.

To backtrack about the bit about 'applied linguistics'. Yet this, of course, is why it is so enormously important for women to write fiction *as* women – it is part of the slow process of decolonialising our language and our basic habits of thought. I really do believe this. It has nothing at all to do with being a 'legislator of mankind' or anything like that; it is to do with the creation of a means of expression for an infinitely greater variety of experience than has been possible heretofore, to say things for which no language previously existed.

One last thing. So there hasn't been a female Shakespeare. Three possible answers: (a) So what. (This is the simplest and best.) (b) There hasn't been a *male* Shakespeare since Shakespeare, dammit. (c) Somewhere, Franz Fanon opines that one cannot, in reason, ask a shoeless peasant in the Upper Volta to write songs like Schubert's; the opportunity to do so has never existed. The concept is meaningless.

The novel, which is my chosen form, has existed as such in Europe for only two or three hundred years. Its existence is directly related to the history of the technology of printing and to the growth of a leisure class with time to read. Much of that leisure class was female and the novel in Western Europe – unlike the forms it has taken when it has been exported to Latin America and Africa in this century – has tended to reflect the preoccupations of the lives of leisured women. Perhaps that's why so many great European novels are about adultery, especially when written by men (*Madame Bovary, Anna Karenina*) who couldn't imagine what else women might get up to if they had a bit of free time. These are interesting historical facts, but they have nothing to do with me as a writer.

One important function of bourgeois fiction is to teach people how to behave in social circles to which they think they might be able to aspire. The novels of Jane Austen are basically fictionalised etiquette lessons and a lot of the fiction that has come directly from the Women's Movement performs, however unconsciously, the same functions. (Marilyn French's *The Women's Room* is really an instruction manual for the older woman post-graduate student.)

But all this bores me stiff, in fact, because it no longer seems particularly relevant to instruct people as to how to behave in a changing society, when one's very existence is instrumental in causing changes the results of which one can't begin to calculate. And I personally feel much more in common with certain Third World writers, both female and male, who are transforming actual fictional forms to both reflect and to precipitate changes in the way people feel about themselves – putting new wine in old bottles and, in some cases, old wine in new bottles. Using fictional forms inherited from the colonial period to create a critique of that period's consequences. Obviously, one is bound to mention Gabriel García Márquez, although he must be getting pretty bored, by this time, to be the white liberal intellectual's pet fabulist, but there are lots of others and some very fine writing, often in a quite conventionally naturalist mode – I'm thinking of the Black South African writer, Bessie Head, who has utilised forms utterly alien to her own historical culture to produce complex illuminations of sexual and political struggle.

But, look, it *is* all applied linguistics. But language is power, life and the instrument of culture, the instrument of domination and liberation.

I don't know. Ten years ago, I'd have said that I, myself, wanted to write stories that could be read by guttering candlelight in the ruins of our cities and still give pleasure, still have meaning. Perhaps I still think that.

All this is very messy and self-contradictory and not very coherent or intelligently argued. It's been amazingly difficult, trying to sort out how I feel that feminism has affected my work, because that is really saying how it has affected my life and I don't really know that because I live my life, I don't examine it. I also feel I've showed off a lot, and given mini-lectures on this and that, in a pompous and middle-aged way. Oh, hell. What I *really* like doing is writing fiction and trying to work things out *that* way.

But I hope this will do.

Chapter 10

WRITING IN A CONTEXT

Noel Greig

From early life I had a picture in my head of 'The Writer'. Male, despite the fact there had always been authors whose work I cherished who were women. 'The Writer' was a calm and serious-minded chap, to whom it did not matter if he worked in a garret by guttering candle-light, or in a solid stone house smelling of polish, with a tall window and a view of a lovely garden. He was well beyond the trivialities of existence, was the wry, pithy, incisive, above all objective commentator on the world and all its follies. He still springs to mind when I'm distracted from the task of writing by a sudden urge to rush to the mirror (am I too old to be putting bleach on my hair?), to the 'phone (who was my lover with last night?), to the newsagent (has that wretched so-and-so, whose rotten play opened last night, got the good reviews I never get?). I irritate myself. Meanwhile, the good calm chap in my head completes another compelling paragraph of original thought and lights a satisfied pipe of tobacco. He's there, I tell you, and he knows I can never completely rid myself of him, even though I have come to understand that his calm, objective creativity depends most likely upon a self-denying wife-secretary beyond the study door. I go back to the typewriter, determined not to allow trivialities access to the creative process. . . .

I'm gazing out of the window. Across the way an elderly woman leans from her own window, places some pot-plants on the ledge. She is often there, looking down at the street and its passers-by. I think she may live on her own in a bedsit. She reminds me of my mother and my mind drifts off in that direction. Her youth was invested in making ends meet, so that I should escape a bleak post-war council estate through a decent grammar-school education and a university degree. Yet the good degree, once achieved, did not propel me into the economic and social way of life that, to her, would have justified the sacrifices. Nor will she have grandchildren – I am an only child – and I know this saddens her. Yet would any future gratification, through children or grandchildren, truly compensate for the fact that she could once have become a professional ballroom dancer? I quibble about 'The Writer' and resist him, yet the plain fact of the matter is that my own bit of freedom in the world comes in large part from the death of my mother's dreams.

Death brings me to war. It is spring, 1982. The Falklands. I hold no sympathy for men who put on uniforms and learn to kill and rape in the service of the state. Yet for me, the ultimate grisly tragedy is the spectacle of young men who could have loved each other, blasting each other out of existence with guns. I want to shout to all those men who march to their deaths in the service of their masters – 'drop your weapons first and then your trousers!'. 'The Writer' is shocked by this cheap gag and reminds me – he is a socialist, by the way – that such glibness totally sidesteps the issues of class, economics and colonialism. I agree with him. I wrote a play recently called *Poppies* in which I put forward an anti-war argument I've not heard from the platforms of power and public debate. I do not want to drop bombs on Russia, because there is a man there I have never met, but one day may. Perhaps we'll make love. I want the option left open.

We do indeed live in a culture that is in love with death, in which the powerful and the privileged – be it class, race or sex – cling onto their top-dog status by fashioning their rapacity and greed into Romance. Flags and victory parades, the desirable gentility of the rich, heroic men with angelic women in tow. They slime us over with their romances, whisper to us that they are right. It has been dreadfully hard, and I think only partially successful, for gay men these past ten years to renounce the privileges (pathetic indeed as some of them are) that the world extends to our sex.

As a playwright, I have never been particularly interested in storming the bastions of the National or the RSC. I've seen some good things there over the years (well, the RSC at any rate) but those institutions disgust me and I'd not care to be part of them. I don't suppose I'll ever meet Peter Hall, but in case he reads this book I'll tell him here: the National's complete lack of commitment to women writers (women anything) stinks. If he believes the National has anything to offer to what is progressive in this society, that's humbug.

Yet my own reactions to the 'large auditoriums' and the desire to seize them – expressed by many male writers I knew in the late 1960s – have often been complex. When those men did express that desire, it was 'The Writer' again, with his broad confidence that he could Speak To The World. The inference that the world was there for him to speak to it. At that time I was busy helping to put together the 'alternative' culture (hate the word as much as anyone but can't find an alternative). In 1967 I took myself off to Brighton with two friends, Ruth Marks and Jenny Harris. In the full flush of the hopes of that time we found an old schoolhouse and set up The Combination. All sorts of people were drawn to the venture, including some of those writers with their eye on the National (quite a lot of them got there, by the way). I denied with every breath the validity of such places, but here's an admission – despite the joys, excitements, optimism and furious creativity of that time, there was often the little nagging doubt that we were creating our own work and theatres because we just weren't up to their grand schemes to dominate the culture. 'Dropping Out' was just as fraught with feelings of inadequacy as 'Coming Out' was later to prove. 'The Writer', 'The Man' kept nagging away in my head.

I am fascinated (angry, frustrated) by these ways in which the 'straight man' I was socialised to become is still there. I wonder if we ever fully recover from that damage. Certainly it was not a case of the gay movement appearing for the feeling of heterosexual men being somehow 'better' to disappear overnight. We (I) tend to drift towards those old, dead ways of getting things done, and the ways we men organised our lives and politics within the gay movement was one of its major discussions. Still is, or should be.

I co-wrote a play called *Men*, with Don Milligan. This

was in the mid-1970s when we both lived in Bradford and were both involved in the local Gay Liberation Front. In differing ways we both tended to be 'leadership' figures. As well as the obvious questions this threw up for the lesbians in the movement, there were often tensions between ourselves and other men in the town, who often felt bulldozed and threatened by our confidence and ability to organise things. *Men* was not strictly autobiographical, being about a successful but closeted shopfloor politico and his campy northern-queen lover, Gene. Richard's unwillingness to link his personal life with his organised political life causes Gene finally to leave. *Men* contributed to the dialogue that was happening in Bradford at the time, not just between gay men and lesbians, but between us and other left and radical groups – groups who often attempted to marginalise our movement, but could not deny its furious vitality in the town (and even nationally) for several years. Its production in Bradford and Leeds is a good example of using a play to speak to a particular, known audience. It was one aspect of a range of talks, barneys, meetings and actions in that community.

Although I have been moved, motivated and educated by some grand-scale work (the Living Theatre, Théâtre du Soleil, large dedicated companies carrying with them a developing radical vision) I do not believe that bigger is necessarily more effective. I certainly think that Dario Fo is robbed of much as soon as his plays are put on by commercial managements hiring actors on the labour-market for West End runs. My blood runs cold when I hear of people I've worked with as colleagues going ga-ga because they've now produced something that is 'transfer material'. Of course we wish to reach people, but to suggest that previously all they had been doing was scratching around for the 'formula' is to trash their own past work.

When Ruth, Jenny and I started up The Combination we placed great emphasis on context. The Combination was never a place where plays were 'consumed', for we shaped up an ambience where theatre was one part of a range of activities and exchanges. When we 'went on the road' after shutting-up-shop in Brighton and before settling in Deptford, our plays were linked to particular issues or struggles. The most effective was probably *The Nab Show*, about the social security system, the final version of which I co-authored with John Turner. This was instrumental in the national Claimants Union movement. So too in Bradford with the General Will theatre company there was the same importance placed on knowing who we were speaking to (more of that later), and of course the same went for Gay Sweatshop. These days, now I'm somewhere between group- or community-based work and freelance writer, I think I tend to address myself to my friends. In the instance of writing, that is, for of course once a play is in performance one's personal resonances take on different meanings. I wrote a play called *The Dear Love of Comrades* for Gay Sweatshop. It was about Edward Carpenter, a nineteenth-century Utopian socialist, and three working-class men, all called George, all of whom were to some degree homosexual. For me, the play was an extension of a dialogue I was having at the time with a small group of close male friends, homo- and heterosexual. It was an addition to an interesting, frustrating, often painful and sometimes loving tangle of power, ambition, jealousy, sex, tenderness and bitterness. The play did not solve anything, of course, though time has resolved much. It was my diary or open letter for that time of nights of conversation and wine, days of phone calls and recriminations. The play was well received and has had a life, so this revelation – somewhat painful to make – may seem irrelevant. The point is, without that very personal jumping-off point I could never have written it. 'The Writer', on the other hand. . . .

Much of the work I have done has been for all-male casts and, having sounded off about the National's track-record on women I know that sounds a bit off. Yet I do know there is a need for us to look at male–male relationships and examine them. One criticism I have of the heterosexual male playwrights who create (often strong and excellent) parts for women is that they're side-stepping the issue. They retain their power, they do not question their privileged positions as inheritors of the main stages. Here's a practical suggestion to all male playwrights – fight for the company you work with to agree, over a time period of, say, twelve months, equal voice, and access to women writers. If you are freelance and have a

commitment to depicting male–male relationships, under-
take an equal distribution at least of female to male parts
when writing for a mixed cast. Companies such as Gay
Sweatshop always operated on this principle of equal access
to resources over a twelve-month period. I'd like to know if
the male writers at the National and RSC are fighting for this
principle.

Bradford was the setting for my 'coming out' as gay, both
as performer and writer. After an alienated year as a freelance director I joined the General Will, a noted left 'agitprop'
group. In Bradford there was already an active discussion
around the question of sexuality and left politics and it was
inevitable that the General Will, already a bit of a cultural
focus in the town, should take this up. I began to edge towards
linking my sexual politics with my work when we constructed a cabaret-show. I developed a bit of a skill for writing
lyrics, and began to use these to take swipes at the notion of
masculinity. Finally there was one about falling in love with
a heterosexual left-wing man, which challenged his attempt
to marginalise sexual politics. That was an important
moment for me as a gay man, and as a performer and a writer,
and I'll never forget singing it for the first time to a huge mob
of students in Belfast, then going off stage and bursting into
tears. After that I took great delight in singing it at the round
of trades clubs, union conferences and International Socialist
do's that formed the 'context' of the General Will's work at the
time.

Yet the context was also heterosexual, and thus irksome,
so it was inevitable that when Bradford GLF expressed a
desire to use theatre as part of its work, I took to the project as
a duck to water. In spring 1975 I worked as scripter with a
large mixed group of lesbians and gay men from the town on
All Het Up, a show designed for a conference on psychiatric
attitudes to homosexuality. It was a huge success and it was a
revelation to me – it was possible to write and perform in a
context that was gay. Later that year I scripted-up another
show with the group, *Present Your Briefs*, for the Sheffield
CHE conference and wrote two songs ('Schizophrenia' and
'All You Gay Women, All You Gay Men') which Bradford
GLF put onto a record alongside the first recorded version of

Tom Robinson's 'Glad To Be Gay'. Before that, however, there occurred an almighty hoo-ha in Bradford. I was still working with the General Will – by this time an Arts Council funded group, though up a bit of a cul-de-sac politically and creatively. The notion of large groups from the community writing and performing their own work had taken off, thanks to GLF, and I suggested that the General Will put its resources at the disposal of this movement and disband its tight-knit 'professional' structure. Actually, 'suggest' is rather too mild a word. There was uproar in the town amongst the left, and I won't go into the desperate, sometimes dreadful things that were said and done. Yet in the midst of it, I did feel that I was taking some kind of revenge on the 'alternative' culture of the 1960s, which I'd had a hand in setting up but which had remained steadfastly heterosexual. I find it difficult and painful to use the word 'revenge' because it seems such a harsh one to put into relation to many people I had worked with and loved (many of whom I still love and still at times work with). Yet that personal element was there for me, in amongst that larger battle for lesbians and gay men to assert their cultural identity. Many people were threatened and much of the left reacted in its time-honoured tradition of getting ratty when the gays get out of order. I was told years later of how the director of a London-based socialist company said at the time 'the queers are taking over in Bradford'.

All this gave me an amazing confidence. There seemed to be no boundaries between personal, political and creative life. Without that vision of such a totally integrated way of living, I don't think I could have approached the two plays about Edward Carpenter I was to write some years later: *Only Connect*, which I co-authored for BBC TV with Drew Griffiths, and *The Dear Love of Comrades*.

Before those plays, however, came *As Time Goes By*, also co-authored with Drew (a working relationship which was one of the most fruitful). *As Time Goes By* was my first association with Gay Sweatshop on my return to London from Bradford (one of the zappiest gay communities in the mid-1970s, we zapped everything in sight, including each other – in fact we often zapped each other clean out of the town. . .). I was scared of *As Time Goes By* because it was epic, had a broad sweep and an overview, all those things I saw the doyens of the new-generation National writers doing so portentously. Yet it was necessary at the time, being the first attempt to portray the lives of different groups of gay men over a century-span. It had a rather large effect, was indeed seminal and was sneered at in the national press.

Just a bit about reviewers here. I hate them. Rather I despise the attempt at 'objectivity' and the only ones I will trust are those who declare their own interests when approaching gay theatre. If they do that then I don't care if the review is bad (well, I do, because the function of a review is to get bums on seats). I admire those who attempt, within the confines of limited space, to give some sort of appreciation of a piece of work, but they are few and far between. I detest the arrogance of large-circulation reviewers who, with a cheap jibe or two, can deny good work access to the public and keep writers and theatre-groups in even worse poverty. It's a male-dominated world, with all its pretensions of knowing-it-all. The worst are the gays who review our work from the safety of their well-carpeted closets.

Only Connect suffered in the same way, although the heaps of letters Drew and I received from viewers compensated for that. An all-male cast again, it was our attempt to show, through the lives and loves of those men, how the ideas and ideals rediscovered in the 1960s, out of which our movement sprang, were directly linked to the hearts and politics of the nineteenth-century Utopian socialists, such as Edward Carpenter and his working-class lovers. It was a lovely chance to get in a dig about the heterosexual appropriation of 'the alternative culture' prior to Gay Liberation.

Although we had a very caring producer for *Only Connect* in W. Stephen Gilbert, I have mixed feelings about writing for television – the faceless organisation, a medium that reeks with polite censorship, the hierarchy. I do believe in collectivity, which is not to say that I am blind to the hierarchy of skills or experience. In the television world the hierarchy of title and rank is very clear. How can a structure so based upon elitism in itself ever be a force for change? For myself, the ideal working situation is in a group where there is some common political and personal ground. I do not care for situations where individuals are hand-picked off the labour-market for what they can 'do' with no regard to what they think and believe.

When I was asked to write this essay I got scared. It seemed too much like becoming 'The Writer' – some sort of look at the work I've done which is credited to me alone, as if everything else was a prelude to that. It's been interesting for me to realise that the collaborative or collective work, particularly that in Bradford with the GLF, the early work with The Combination, has equal creative and political validity for me. In the end, it's the personal relationships, the shared insights that come from working with people that are sustaining, and that can happen whether it's putting on a half an hour's street theatre on the steps of Camden Town Hall or presenting a group of colleagues with an 'all my own work' script. I've noticed too that I've concentrated on that work which has been about men, although I have and do work alongside many women and some of those relationships are both creatively and personally very dear to me. Perhaps I have written this to them, for if I continue to write, in whatever capacity, it will only be on the basis of a developing set of work-friendship relationships. There are, I know, enormous problems around the question of women working with men, yet I believe and hope that these are not insurmountable. I'd like this essay to be able to contribute to the process of our understanding of each other, and so aid that work.

Chapter 11

ART, FEMINISM AND CRITICISM

Rozsika Parker

My mother's desk was in the sitting room when I was a child. She wrote constantly with an ability to concentrate which infuriated her six children. She appeared deaf to us. Screams, squabbles and demands for arbitration simply glanced off her. Predictably, imitation and identification with the mother for me meant not cooking, cleaning or sewing but writing. While other girls pushed brooms about or stood on chairs at the kitchen sink, hands in the washing-up bowl, I was covering pages with looped squiggles – my 'writing', to be accorded absolute privilege and priority.

Although having a mother who wrote professionally enabled me to view the identity 'writer' as appropriate for women, it by no means rendered writing unproblematic. Like all mother/daughter relationships, ours was fraught with ambivalence; I was identified with my mother but at the same time sought differentiation and separation. I was to be a writer but, at all costs, not a writer in the same mould as my mother.

My mother's autocratic and idiosyncratic personality, however, ensured emulation while forbidding competition. She is a scientist. She split her skills between her oldest children, according to their gender. My brother was to be a scientist and I was to write. We both conformed to parental direction and social expectation. He read biochemistry at university while my degree was in the history of art.

Art criticism and the history of art were areas in which women had already carved a place for themselves. Writing about art had long been deemed an acceptable occupation for 'ladies'. Recording and responding to the work of artists was seen as a receptive, sensitive, appreciative, thoroughly feminine activity. However, the writers of art history and criticism do wield power, shaping our view of history and creating a scale of cultural values. But in the hands of women, the particular power could be contained and categorised as maternal power – rewarding, encouraging and nurturing artists. As in other areas, the ideology of 'fit work for women' opened the door of the discipline to women – once inside, some radically departed from the feminine ideal of behaviour while others conformed to it. I, of course, knew nothing of the history of women in the history of art when I decided to read the subject at university. I thought my decision was determined by my O and A Levels and a vague sense that it was a 'safe' subject, suitably distanced from science, my mother and brother.

When I left university I wanted to write and to obtain some reviewing work. However, I found myself at odds with the role of conventional critic, and the complex hierarchical structure that knits critic, artist, art market, art work and audience. The critic has today assumed an unprecedented importance, reconsidering and assessing the theories and premises upon which modern art is based. Her or his voice is that of authority, though nevertheless dependent upon and considered secondary to the artist, who in turn needs critical notice to survive professionally. Attracting the attention of private galleries and the support of public funding is helped by favourable press notices. The division of labour between artist and critic sets up a curious dynamic of mutual need and distrust. There are, though, ways in which the hostility is modified or dispelled. Critics become committed to particular artists or art movements, promoting, defending and mediating the work to the public. Also, boundaries and hierarchies between artists, writers and curators become blurred by social events which structure the art world: the private views, press lunches and openings when the different sides meet.

I found myself expected to speak with the voice of authority amidst these curious contradictions and antagonisms. I couldn't do it. Was I on the side of the artist or the audience? Who did I want to please, the artist or the magazine editor? Predictably I produced the most turgid

form of art criticism – art appreciation – paralleling the work
of art in appreciative prose. Adverbs, adjectives and somewhat breathless hyperbole allowed space for very little else.

Had it not been for the re-emergence of feminism in the
late 1960s I would have undoubtedly abandoned my ambition
to write. Feminism produced a radical critique and re-
assessment of the relationship between artist, critic and
audience, while transforming art practice itself. And, of
crucial importance for me, feminism offered a new forum for
women writers – *Spare Rib*.

In 1971 I read the pre-launch publicity for the magazine.
The aim to bring feminism to women's attention through a
traditional feminine format – the women's magazine – but
transformed by a new feminist journalism, was a political
and publishing venture I entirely supported. I wrote to the
editors, Rosie Boycott and Marsha Rowe, asking for work.
Soon afterwards I nervously climbed a narrow staircase to a
small, bright yellow office near Carnaby Street. 'I'll do anything,' I said, 'though in fact there is not much I can do. I know
nothing of magazine production and have little experience of
writing and none of editing.' Conventional magazine editors
would have shown me back down the narrow staircase but
the feminist insistence that all skills can be learned by every
woman got me a job. I was to be responsible for coverage of the
visual arts and was delegated some editorial work.

Out of the plethora of London-based independent magazines which emerged during the late 1960s and early 1970s,
Spare Rib is one of the two survivors and the only one to
maintain the structure which was established about a year
after I joined the magazine. (Here I am concerned only to
convey my own experience of writing on art in the context of
Spare Rib. A proper appraisal of the magazine's aims and
achievements cannot be the work of an individual but rather
the sifting, sorting and collating of the group memory.) We
functioned as a collective with no hierarchy and equal pay for
all. *Spare Rib* was committed to breaking down the traditional conditions of magazine production. Members of the
collective were expected to learn every aspect of production
from editing to design and distribution. The relationship
between editor and contributor, reviewer and reviewed were

to be placed on a new, more equal footing. Women who had never written before were encouraged to start – working closely with editors who were to learn to facilitate rather than dictate style and content. That was the ideal. Of course it was never entirely achieved. The constraints and contradictions of bringing out a ludicrously undercapitalised magazine on a commercial basis in a conventional market, constantly cut across our intentions. Nevertheless, our determination to achieve a feminist, collective mode of living and working in a competitive, non-feminist, even anti-feminist world, provoked real changes in our way of writing and producing a magazine.

I was no longer in a position of ambiguous authority when writing on the visual arts. The democratic ideals of 1970s feminism put an end to that, but also my relationship to the artists whose work I encountered was entirely changed. Conferences, workshops, study groups and panel discussions in conjunction with exhibitions cut across traditional divisions amongst workers in the visual arts. Art historians, graphic designers, publishers, poster-makers, photographers, film-makers, textile artists and gallery visitors exchanged experiences and identified common problems and ambitions. I found myself in alliance with women artists – united in an attempt to bring feminist ideas to as wide a public as possible.

Moreover, feminist art practice changed the mediating role of the critic. Feminist artists expect women to bring their own experiences to bear on the art, recognising the meanings of the materials used and the full implication of the content in terms of their own lives. Feminists work with the raw materials of the construction of femininity. Their subject matter has ranged from childbirth and pregnancy to make-up, advertising, cooking, menstruation, shopping, and the sexual division of labour in industry: 'In feminist art we are dealing with the way in which the meanings, the patterns of understanding which we are struggling to produce can be made vivid for the audience.' Communication is thus of central concern to feminist artists – they do not look to critics to explain their work. Nevertheless, critics are needed to contextualise and draw attention to it.

My first article on feminist art for *Spare Rib* focussed on the Women's Workshop of the Artists' Union, founded in 1972. I attended workshop meetings, I read their manifesto, wrote the article and gave it to the group to read prior to publication. They discussed it and delivered their verdict: 'It's colour supplement journalism.' I was crushed. Mary Kelly, then chairperson of the Union, sat down with me and worked through the article, toughening and tightening it up. The punch and the politics had been lost in my attempt to produce popular journalism. The final version was direct, informative and today provides a useful view of a particular moment in the history of feminist art practice.

Although in that case the group's judgment was correct, in those days I was too swayed by criticism, too anxiously ready to change my work on demand. At *Spare Rib* every article was to be read and commented upon by each member of the collective. As editor or writer on the receiving end of a sheaf of notes often containing widely disparate responses, it was imperative to learn to delve into damning comments, distinguishing the grinding of individual axes from appropriate criticism. It was only after years of working collectively that I learned how to respond confidently.

Learning to collaborate collectively rather than to meekly capitulate was relatively easy in comparison to the other major problem I faced. My sense of alliance with feminist artists and my awareness of the hostility that existed towards feminist art ('if it's political it's not art') made it hard to voice negative criticism of that art. My solution was rather than simply passing judgment, to attempt to convey the artist's intentions and to record the work's effect, relating it to feminist theory generally. That form of reviewing is valid – yet not sufficient. 'I want to know what you think and feel about it,' complained one woman. I replied that my role was to enable others to get a handle on the work for themselves. 'But I need criticism,' she persisted.

Clearly difficulties do exist between feminist artists as individuals and writers on feminist art even though there is infinitely more communication and debate amongst them than in the conventional art world. Some feminists object to individual reviews and monographs on the grounds that they reproduce the conditions of the art market which has been so oppressive to women, fostering competition, forwarding the myth of the artist as singular and solitary genius, and ultimately functioning primarily as part of publicity machinery. Other feminists believe that rejecting reviews of individuals' work makes for the invisibility of feminist artists.

Griselda Pollock, writing in the British *Feminist Art News* brings together all the strands:

> Writing about feminist art is both difficult and treacherous. In the wake of the changes in feminist art wrought by a new political consciousness, writing about art has to change similarly. Yet feminist are is made by women whose livelihood depends directly or indirectly upon their work. . . . As artists women have been excluded from both the publicity – critics rarely discuss art by women – and from the mythic status of Great Artist – women artists are not recorded by art history. . . . So women artists justifiably want recognition as creative individuals both in their profession and on behalf of all women. But the art that the women's movement has generated has been the product of a political movement committed to collectivity, to the avoidance of the star and the rejection of the token woman.

The criticism levelled at feminist writers by feminist artists, for not adequately covering individuals and their work, has to be viewed in the light of the political radicalisation of writing about feminist practices in terms of their content and not their authors. This is in marked contrast to the conventional press which considers a show worthy of notice according to the fame or infamy of the artist.

When writing about the autumn of women's exhibitions in 1980 I concentrated entirely on the heterogeneous character of the feminist work on view, the widely different artistic strategies adopted by the exhibitions. In response, American artist May Stevens wrote a critical letter to the magazine pointing out that in all I had mentioned five women's names in the article and not one of them was an artist. (They were in fact the friends whose help I acknowledged in a footnote.) On the one hand my response was a sulky, self righteous 'and all I've done for feminism' and on the other hand I did see her point. As Adrienne Rich put it, the feminist critic should address her comments to the feminist artist or writer whose work she reviews. Yet feminist writing is often intended to enlighten a wide public on the tactics and strategies of the women artists' movement. Ideally the two approaches should be complementary, not in conflict. That a conflict exists is a symptom of the contradictions feminists face in trying to negotiate a space for feminist cultural work in and against the existing division of labour and the myth of the artist.

One outcome of the situation is that feminist artists have themselves begun to write extensively about their own and each other's work, curating their own shows, collating their own catalogues and interviewing one another. Extraordinarily interesting and important work has been produced. But as Jacqueline Morreau, one of the organisers of the exhibition *Women's Images of Men* (1980) said to me, 'I have no time to go to the studio, no time for my own painting.'

Interviews have proved a particularly fruitful way of airing debates around feminist art. Thus, for example, Monica Ross and Kate Walker, two artists who worked together on the travelling exhibition *Fenix*, produced and printed a discussion on the major issues of the show, explaining why they worked on the exhibition *in situ* rather than presenting a finished spectacle.

As the numbers of feminist artists grew and the numbers of people and publications prepared to record their work remained extremely limited, *Spare Rib* came under considerable pressure to publish more articles on art. It presented the collective with a conflict I shared. The great attraction of writing on art for *Spare Rib* was that it brought the visual arts to the attention of an audience infinitely wider than that reached by specialist art publications. Unlike other radical movements, the Women's Liberation Movement has never dismissed the arts as a diversion, but rather recognised the significance of the arts in maintaining male dominance; and acknowledged the importance of feminist artists constructing a view of the world consciously from their positioning as women. Regular coverage of the visual arts was an innovation for a women's magazine: it signified *Spare Rib's* early determination to go beyond subjects deemed acceptable in women's magazines. However, in our society the visual arts are not 'popular' and *Spare Rib* is a magazine committed to engaging a large cross-class readership. Although feminist art is a more socially oriented, communicative kind of art, coverage of the arts was in competition with articles relating to every aspect of women's lives from sexuality to equal pay.

During editorial meetings I would announce, 'I'd like two double-page spreads for the visual arts feature.' Silence followed. 'The pictures could then be a generous size,' I would add, trying to sound and to feel encouraging. The collective was in a dilemma. The demand for column inches, let alone double-page spreads, was intense, and art is predominantly a middle-class, elitist practice – that is what feminists are committed to change. The conflict was sometimes debilitating but it forced us to develop new, more accessible ways of writing on the arts, constantly questioning language and style. 'Light but powerful' was the phrase coined to express our ideal.

I worked for *Spare Rib* for ten years – latterly on a part-time basis – editing and writing articles not only on the arts but on a wide spectrum of issues, in particular psychology and psychotherapy. I stopped working full-time for the magazine in order to write a book with Griselda Pollock: *Old Mistresses: Women, Art and Ideology* (Routledge & Kegan Paul, 1981) was a continuation of our work in the Women's Art History Collective. I followed it up with *The Subversive Stitch: Embroidery and the Making of the Feminine*. Whereas writing on the visual arts in *Spare Rib* sometimes resembled sending messages to sea in a bottle, an art history book could be aimed at a smaller but more defined audience. And, as importantly for myself and Griselda Pollock, with thousands of words at our disposal, rather than the hundreds available for an article, we found it possible to take issue with existing feminist theory, rather than constantly defending feminism in a hostile world. At present we are working on a book which is to be an anthology of writings about women, art and feminism in Britain, and a history of the women's art movement during the 1970s.

Prior to the resurgence of feminism I had attributed my difficulties in writing about art purely to my personal and particular inability to negotiate the division of labour between artist, writer and audience. My problems did of course relate to my own psyche, but feminism taught me to see also the wider perspective. I came into contact with a range of women who were developing analyses of the conditions of art practice and were determined to transform them. Looking back at the past ten years I find myself swinging between sentimentality and frustration, between defeatism and the making of extravagant claims. All I can say with certainty is that feminism provided a forum and purpose, while the ideology of collectivity enabled me to write.

Chapter 12

THROUGH THE LOOKING GLASS

Alison Hennegan

For just over four years of my life I was, in one sense, unique. From June 1977 until August 1981 I was the only journalist in Great Britain paid to write as a lesbian.

I joined *Gay News* as an utter novice, journalistically speaking. The credentials I brought to half of my job, Assistant Features Editor (a post whose first holder I was), came from my five years, previous experience in the gay movement where I had worked primarily in the areas of befriending and counselling. My claims to the other half of my title, Literary Editor, were rooted in a Cambridge English degree, an uncompleted PhD thesis on homosexual literature, and fifteen years of voracious but focussed reading of books by, for and about gay people.

I was twenty-nine years of age and it was my first full-time job. My belief in the necessity and value of a gay movement in which men and women worked together was firm (hence my willingness to work with *Gay News*, a theoretically 'mixed' paper) but defensive (I carried for years a deep-seated but not always clearly acknowledged sense of guilt and inferiority in the presence of lesbians working in women-only or lesbian-only enterprises). My attitude to feminism was at that time a mass of painful confusions. At its heart was a suspicion that *I* didn't want *it*, coupled with the certainty that *it* didn't want *me*.

Despite the claims so often made by anti-feminists that feminism is 'riddled' with lesbians who insist on making life beastly for 'real [heterosexual] women', my own experience was very much other. Somewhere, somehow, I had formed a hazy but tenacious impression that feminism was essentially concerned to solve the problem of men-and-women-*together* rather than to achieve the peaceful, parallel co-existence which was my own aim. Lesbians, I was told, got in the way and muddled things up, deflecting much-needed energy and thought from the 'real' problems of 'real' women. The implicit assumption that lesbians weren't real women found answering echoes in my own assessment of myself. With hindsight I can see that from my mid-teens I had assumed my membership of 'the third sex', without ever having heard the phrase. As an undergraduate in the late 1960s I began to cross-dress: shirts, collars, cuff-links, watch-chains and buttonholes – a mixture of *fin-de-siècle* nostalgia, sixties fun and an alarmingly serious personal search for style, identity and a statement of difference.

Some seven years later, when I joined *Gay News*, my dress was much modified but the gay man in my head flourished as vigorously as ever. Hardly surprising, then, that I faced the prospect of joining the paper (supposedly mixed but in fact a self-consciously male publication) with no qualms other than those about my as yet untried journalistic competence.

No raw novice could have hoped for a more intelligent, kindly and stimulating teacher. Never once did Keith Howes (the Features Editor) register, by even so much as a carefully suppressed wince, a hint of impatience for what, looking back, I can see were blunders. Steadily he began to put me through a range of testing assignments. There were interviews with seemingly inappropriate subjects (Arnold Schwarzenegger came early on) and articles on topics seemingly more suitable for other pens to dwell on (I remember still a really rather good piece on the history and practice of penile enlargement: it made me some unexpected male friends and nearly lost me some female ones).

Then there were theatre reviews. One of Divine's (the vaguely male transvestite actor) repulsively unfunny Trash orgies, set in a women's prison, was the first. I wrote my review as any woman might. I took it for granted that however anxious an audience may be to prove itself sophisticated in the Aesthetics of Trash, there really isn't anything funny, for a woman with even half her brain working, in ninety minutes of ritualised rape, brutalisation,

humiliation and murder. I didn't understand at the time why
Keith drew in his breath sharply, then grinned before
handing it to the Editor, saying 'Yes, well, I don't think we've
carried a review of Divine quite like *that* before!' The Editor,
Denis Lemon, agreed, grinned and sent it off to the type-
setters.

Later, various (male) readers explained – by letter and in
person – that, unfortunately, I hadn't actually *understood*
about Trash. It was the first of many instances when I 'failed'
to understand. I didn't understand that pornography is liber-
ating (*always*); that sado-masochism is the only path to true
freedom; that anything which questions the sacred right of
gay men to fuck where and when (though not always whom)
they like is an intolerable assault upon the freedom of the
individual; that it's *fun* to be a sex object; that it's *friendlier* to
call women 'girls'; that women readers of *Gay News* must not
complain of display advertisements showing bulging
crutches but male readers were delicate flowers who must be
shielded from the knowledge that women menstruate; that
it's an intolerable curtailment of individual freedom to
suggest that your individual freedom has been curtailed if
you're subjected to unwanted sexual advances; that it's silly
to be offended if a gay man says 'Anyone for rape?'; and,
finally, of course, that the trouble with lesbians is they get so
serious about things.

By no means all male readers responded in that way. But
somehow I couldn't help noticing that every reader who did
was male. Many male readers, however, were familiar with
and espoused the aims and arguments of the Women's Movement. For them there could be no gay liberation without
women's liberation. They applauded and encouraged my
feminism as exemplified in my work. Which gave me quite a
shock. Me? A *feminist*?

Well, yes. I don't know *why* it took me so long to realise
that my own beliefs and needs were those of feminism. I don't
know, either, why it took so long to see that in many respects
Gay News was deeply antipathetic to them. Despite my close
and loving relationships with individual men on the staff, the
paper itself was deeply suspicious of women. The reasons,
I believe, were a mixture. There was the commercial

argument: what will happen to our mainly gay-male ghetto display advertisers and our more overtly erotic material if we get too many women readers? There was the historical argument: all efforts of gay men and women to work together in true equality have failed – Gay Liberation Front in the early 1970s; *Gay News* itself in the very beginning; the Campaign for Homosexual Equality, always. It's too risky and, anyway, we know it's doomed. And finally there was the teasing question of sexual temperament. After all, at the risk of sounding ludicrously banal, it seems fair to say that all homosexual people have decided that, at some very basic level, the other sex simply Will Not Do. My earlier political position had been based on a belief that gay women and men had more to unite them than to divide them. During my first few years at *Gay News* I began dimly and painfully to realise that I had underestimated the importance of our differences.

Gradually I began to understand the reasons for old problems and to foresee new ones. Writing, or to be more precise, nerving myself to write, has always been a torment to me. I began to see some of the reasons why. As the only woman journalist on the paper, each time I wrote it was as '*the* lesbian'. With each article, each interview, I felt enormous (but until recently unarticulated) pressure to make it the definitive lesbian piece. (Whatever *that* might be.)

On the other hand I did not feel free to write *to* lesbians. Our readership was mixed but mainly male. To whom, *for* whom was I to write? For the male majority? For lesbians, with no punches pulled, no apologies for the way I saw the world, and trusting that men of sufficient good will and intellectual curiosity would also read me? Or was I to write to some strange homogeneous abstraction called 'the gay community' and, as with all such abstractions, supposedly bi-gendered but actually male? Morever, in those many areas where I had complete freedom of choice what was I to write about? I became prey to a constant self-questioning about whether a subject or person (for 'person' read 'woman') was 'worthy' to be drawn to the readers' (for 'readers' read 'male') attention. The doubts remained even when the subjects were women whose work and example had been of crucial significance in my own life and that of many other lesbians.

My problem, in fact, was 'finding my voice' or learning how to break silence. It's a subject with which many women authors have particularly concerned themselves recently: Adrienne Rich in *Lies, Secrets and Silence*; Susan Griffin in *Pornography and Silence*; Tillie Olsen in *Silences*. I have interviewed them all for *Gay News* over the past few years and tried to use the resulting articles to exemplify and begin to solve the difficulties which I, as writer, and other lesbians, as readers, face in *Gay News*.

I never expressed these doubts at the time. I hadn't even expressed them to myself. I was in an altogether unfamiliar state of bewilderment and muddle which worried and nagged at me. Keith Howes left as Features Editor in the late autumn of 1979. As Editor, Denis Lemon took over the features section. I found it even harder to offer topics which would be of particular interest to women readers and to me as a writer who was a woman.

A partial solution to my unvoiced conflict came with Denis Lemon's suggestion that as Literary Editor I should create a Literary Supplement for the paper – a guaranteed eight pages every fortnight to use as I thought best. For me the results were helpful and strengthening. (And, leaving false modesty aside, I don't think the paper was the loser, either.) I might be the wrong gender to work at *Gay News* and I might have the wrong politics to be a proper lesbian feminist but I *did* know a damn sight more about books than anybody else on the paper and quite a lot more than most people outside it. Note the insidious invoking of Expert Status. Politically impure, maybe, but it gave me a much-needed boost of confidence, restored to me an area in which I could claim that my (female) sense of the interesting, the noteworthy, the relevant was as good as any (male) body's.

I worked to make sure that those eight pages were of equal interest to men and women; to make sure that *pictures* of women abounded (page after page of *Gay News* carried no female images at all); I plucked up my courage to invite women who I knew had little reason to feel kindly towards the paper to review and write for me and I never quite got over the little shock of surprise and pleasure when they accepted.

In those pages – and nowhere else in the paper – women and men had an equal voice. Or, as a gay male journalist writing for *the* liberal Daily said, my pages were showing 'a marked feminist bias'. For, as we all know, giving women their due is giving them too much. As the paper underwent various changes of editorial direction and of size, the literary pages have been progressively cut. With *Gay News* now (January 1983) a mere forty pages where once there were fifty-six, only two can be spared for books and authors. The lessons learned, however, in those more spacious days remain: of them the most important is that in a mixed publication only women will safeguard women's interests.

In August 1981 I stopped being unique. A second woman, Gill Hanscombe, joined *Gay News*. Her title – Staff Reporter – gave no indication of her past work as poet, novelist and critic. Her advent was to be of the greatest importance to me. Much that had been unclear and unarticulated fell into place. I began to see my recent past in the mirror of another woman's experience, began to see that my reactions to certain values, standards and assumptions were not idiosyncratically (and slightly madly) unique; rather, they were part of a female reaction to a male world. It was and is invaluable, strengthening – and very painful because it made it impossible to ignore the fact that a woman working at *Gay News* was inevitably engaged in a constant battle waged around gender.

I became aware of the confidence (often unjustified) with which male colleagues advanced their vision of the world. I watched, disbelieving and embarrassed at the naked egotism with which one of them pushed his own material. I discovered that men who prided themselves on the fact that 'all my best friends are dykes' felt perfectly comfortable about telling me that I wasn't really a lesbian. One male colleague drove the final point home in an argument with me by asserting that he knew more about lesbians than I did, anyway.

Perhaps those men felt themselves goaded into such incautious nonsenses because of other changes happening in the paper. Late in 1981 *Sappho*, the lesbian monthly magazine, had died. A number of its subscribers wrote to Denis Lemon asking him to guarantee specifically lesbian space in *Gay News*. There were editorial discussions and an open meeting with *Sappho* readers. February 1982 saw the first appearance of 'The Visible Lesbian', one page (which rapidly became two) of purely lesbian material, collectively edited by *all* the women working at *Gay News*, whatever their jobs.

The collective has complete autonomy over contents (subject only to the workings of the libel laws), and each woman has an equal voice. The experience of working together gave us a strong sense of group identity. The process I had already begun with Gill Hanscombe widened and deepened – for me, for her, for all of us. The phrase 'the GN women' became current in house, sometimes jocularly, sometimes purely descriptively, sometimes exasperatedly. Some of the men who knew more about lesbians than I did left.

In the autumn of 1982 *Gay News* became embroiled in seemingly intractable ownership tangles and financial crises. Redundancies affecting almost half the workforce were demanded. They fell particularly heavily on the women. The staff, acting as a federated Chapel, were successful in resisting them, only to enter a protracted period of managerial confusion and uncertainty. As I write, I do not know whether the paper will exist for more than a few weeks. I *do* know that if *Gay News* dies received wisdom in certain quarters will explain it like this: 'Well, you see, *Gay News* was OK until the women started getting uppity. They got above themselves. You know, give 'em an inch and . . . well. . . . You mark my words, it was the lesbians who killed *Gay News*.'

On two counts it will be a cruelly unjust perversion of the truth. First, because looking back over my five and a half years at *Gay News* I can see that for most of the time women have been merely tolerated and then only if they accepted a secondary role which bore no relation to their abilities. It is always shocking to hear the weak blamed when the strong act against them.

And second, because it is precisely the energy, endurance and vision shown by its women and those of its men who recognise and support their struggle which could save *Gay News*, if only its owners would allow them to.

Chapter 13

THE EL VINO MENTALITY

Andrew Lumsden

My grandfather edited a northern newspaper in the Rothermere group; my father was briefly a reporter with the *Daily Mail* in the 1930s. Through my father's friendships in Fleet Street, I got a job as a financial reporter with the *Daily Telegraph* in 1963. I was twenty-one, and remained a journalist successively with the *Telegraph*, *Management Today*, and *The Times*, until I was thirty-one, when I resigned. At the beginning of that career I supposed myself to be a heterosexual who in due course would marry and have children; at the end of it, I knew I was homosexual and had been 'out' professionally for two years.

My interiorised oppression brought out none of the brilliance and wit which sexual inhibition is sometimes supposed to provoke. The failure to understand my own sexual wishes made me feel entirely detached from my occupation, and from any ambitions within it. I didn't despise journalism itself, which I saw as having more to do with entertainment than with literature, but I couldn't regard myself as belonging to journalism. The inner attitude of observer, rather than true participant, on the whole goes down very well with employers. When I decided to leave the *Telegraph* I was asked to stay; but also the *Sunday Telegraph*, *The Times,* and *Management Today* all asked me to join them. I said no to *The Times* at first, then yes two years later.

Those years seem to me fascinating from a 'positive vetting' point of view. It must have been plain to some in 1963–9, when I was aged between twenty-one and twenty-eight, that I was an unaware homosexual. My laten homosexuality made no difference to my career prospects on any of the newspapers. I could have gone fairly high in national newspapers – not to an Editorship, I think, but to the minor celebrity of a known writer and head of department. My close colleagues would have been quite aware that I was homosexual, even if it was never discussed. I might perhaps have had a live-in lover, and exchanged occasional hospitality with married colleagues and other discreet homosexuals in London's professional world. Had a scandal ever broken out – had I been taken to court for cottaging or for relations with an under twenty-one-year-old – my colleagues and employers would have tried to minimise the damage, and to keep me in my job.

None of this happened. There would have been a price, and it was one I can't pay. I say 'can't', without any affectations of moral grandeur. If I'd been aware of my own homosexuality from adolescence, and none the less gone into Fleet Street, I would have adapted myself in the course of the 1960s to the divorce between private life and employed life which is customary for tens of thousands, if not perhaps for millions, of gays in all occupations. From the time, beginning 1968–9, when the consciousness rose in me that this unknown kind of person, a homosexual, was almost certainly what I was, it was evident to me that I was going to confess my discovery, shout about it. Shock there certainly was, and dismay at having to re-make my emotional and sexual life, as if pubescence had arrived when I was almost thirty; but more than anything else I remember the intellectual thrill. I watched myself centring in a drama which I only later learned to call 'coming out'.

I have pointed out, in *Gay News* and on radio programmes, that there are no truly 'out' homosexual journalists in mainstream British press and media, and I call this censorship. In 1982 a BBC radio interviewer asked me what difference would be made to the reporting of, say, Middle East politics if a correspondent were an 'out' homosexual. Peter Hillmore, of *The Observer*, on the same programme, was critical of the 'ghetto' mentality which proposes a gay vantage-point on every aspect of human life (though, interestingly, it was necessary, perhaps for the first time in British broadcasting, for the BBC to specify that Hillmore is heterosexual, a matter which listeners would ordinarily be expected to take entirely for granted). I know perfectly well than an out gay foreign correspondent for the BBC or *The Times* wouldn't produce quite the same copy that an out heterosexual does, but proving it isn't an easy matter. If fish are the last to notice that they swim in water, so Fleet Street and the broadcasting media are the last to notice that they swim in a heterosexual element, which they mistake for the professional objective of impartiality. No aware homosexual could be stationed in the Middle East, or in Israel, without a consciousness that all the regimes are corrupted in their sexual as in their other attitudes, and would place a higher importance on the fact than the heterosexual reporter. It is impossible to be employed to voice your perceptions and for those perceptions to be uninfluenced by your gender or your orientation. The question is whether the influence should be tacit or overt, 'closeted' or 'out'.

I was still on *The Times* when I started to acknowledge my homosexuality. Not much room, in that field of stocks and shares and price-earnings ratios and the computer revolution, for declared sexual orientation; or so it would seem. I stayed on *The Times* for another three years, up to autumn 1972, during which I continued to be a financial journalist, but with my new, delighted, sexual self-knowledge. I made my self-discovery public. No one attempted to dismiss me, or even to remove my bye-line from the paper. I had quite consciously banked on its being impossible, in the new liberalism of the 1960s, for such a world newspaper as *The Times* to be seen firing a journalist because he had gone on television and written openly elsewhere, as I did, of being gay. Unfortunately, I was left, on *The Times*, with the same inexpressive writing task as before, that of financial journalist. I had had a revolution in personality which could find no reflection in my writing.

I can see now how any quality paper could make very responsible use of a homosexual financial journalist. He or she could specialise in personal savings and finance as it affects the single individual and the single parent or the various legal groupings of unmarried persons. Even if old-fashioned stereotyping of gay interests is set aside, it's probably true that such a journalist would be particularly good at writing about the financial worlds of fashion, fine art and entertainment, which get virtually no serious attention from the financial pages, even though the product in these three areas is so profoundly affected by the little-discussed financial structures. An undeclared tendency to see a gender-expertise in the journalism of personal savings and finance had appeared, long before 1969, in the reputations achieved by a number of women financial journalists, though shunting them aside from the main promotion ladders may have had something to do with this.

However, at the time I resigned from the paper. There seemed to be nothing that I could aim to do in any branch of the established media which could make use of the intellectual brilliance which I saw in the 'gay revolution' itself, or which could employ any talents of mine which sprang from my true personality. At times in later years, when I was poor or doing nothing of use to myself or anyone, I often questioned the decision. It seemed to me that I'd thrown away a chance to make myself uniquely useful to gay people, and specifically to the ruining of gay male stereotypes. While still on *The Times* I'd prompted a *Panorama* programme on television about Gay Liberation Front, told the Editor of *The Times* (William Rees-Mogg) about it, and obtained his consent to appear on it. I'd also had his consent to write about one of the homosexual issues of the day in one of the British political weeklies (though I gathered afterwards that he hadn't expected me to declare my own homosexuality in the course of the article). I could have become a token of how you can get away with it, even at the heart of the Establishment. And over time, I have little doubt, the spectacle would have had an effect on the thousands of journalists whose orientation remains a secret from readers, viewers and listeners; or, worse, from their own working colleagues.

The sheer chronological accident that my personal coming out coincided not only with the arrival in England of American Gay Liberation movement, but also with my working for so dignified an institution as *The Times*, had an unexpected effect on the facilities for openly gay writing that opened up in Britain in the 1970s. At meetings of Gay Liberation Front in London in 1971, I, who was longing to cease to be a journalist, met and talked with Denis Lemon, who was longing to become one. The admiration I'd conceived over six or seven years for the best qualities of 'straight' journalism – its theory of objectivity, its 'show must go on' determination to get a paper to the reader – made me critical of the necessarily episodic and polemical papers that GLF and others were putting out. I respected them for what they were, without believing that they could ever answer the needs (as I saw them) of tens of thousands of homosexuals who would never happily define themselves as 'political', let alone as socially revolutionary; or who might learn to be so, but not unless information was regularly and entertainingly supplied to them without prior editorial choice of what was in some sense or other correct. The straight press did enough prior censorship of what is sexually correct. It seemed desirable that there should be a range of politically partisan papers for lesbians and gay men – *plus* at least one nationally-distributed newspaper produced by and for both sexes of homosexuals; and competitive in the market-place alongside other periodicals. The suggestion of such a newspaper was uneasily received. To many it contradicted the polemical impetus which had briefly made Gay Liberation Front so vast a force for change in the homosexual population of Britain. It explicitly jettisoned, from the proposed editorial policy, every commitment except to describe what gay men and women were saying and doing. It was not to begin and operate under an analytic strategy, gay Marxist, 'genderfuck', or even, in any meaningful sense, feminist. It would be the vehicle for what others were doing and thinking, with the sole stipulation that it mirror their doings and sayings as faithfully as possible. The title eventually chosen, *Gay News*, was deliberately the bluntest possible expression of what form of journalism the paper would be expected to provide. Very privately, for my own satisfaction, it was also a symbolic naming – the antithesis of the name of that part of *The Times* for which I was less and less willingly working: *Times Business News*.

Gay News became a forum for openly homosexual writing the like of which had never before been seen in Britain – but not for me. In fact, I withdrew from the project of

Gay News before the first issue came out in summer 1972. I was already sleeplessly walking the West End in the small hours of the morning trying to accept that for my sanity I *must* leave *The Times* and journalism. I could neither work on *The Times* and the *Gay News* project simultaneously, nor could I imagine leaving *The Times* and moving directly into a still more arduous journalistic enterprise, even if it was by homosexuals, for homosexuals. I have often thought what a beautiful career mine could have been, a successful journalist on the straight press who learnt to know himself as gay, and promptly founded a paper, *Gay News*, in which he could express himself naturally, and write for those most desperately in need of information. Out of such perfect conjunctions of sudden awareness, a renunciation, and new creation are saints made. But it took me six years, until 1978, to feel stirring in me anything I might wish to say as an integrated personality, both journalist and homosexual. Even then, my efforts were stumbling, amateurish, and remained unpublished.

I feel sometimes that only in Britain could the fate of a national newspaper journalist who broke all taboos in 1970–1 have aroused no subsequent curiosity from the intellectual life of the country. A pathic, I used to say, has no honour in his own country. This was largely self-pitying, since no one forced me to leave regular journalism or to abandon *Gay News*, but there is an element of justice in the criticism. There is a complete absence of true interest in the redefinition of lesbian and gay male self-consciousness – an event without real equivalent, and with extreme repercussions for heterosexual self-definition. Gay civil rights gets a degree of attention that would have seemed impossible fifteen years ago, yes; but the homosexual voice, the trained voice of the out lesbian or gay man whose sensual and intellectual self-awareness have at last come together in as integrated a form as any out heterosexual, that no. If Radio 3, the *Listener*, the *Times Literary Supplement, Encounter*, the serious review sections of the quality papers, BBC 2, *Books & Bookmen*, and a handful of other media are to be taken as representing the non-party-political outlets of the country's intellectual life, all are barred, in effect, to such people as myself. They employ, or turn for contributions to, a large number of men and women whose homosexuality isn't declared to the readership or audience; but the person whose sexual orientation will infallibly be made explicit whenever the context warrants it is always a heterosexual. This is a truth which has to be felt. Publishers and programmers have little conscious awareness of the policy they pursue. Many are themselves gay, openly so within the workplace, but feel themselves to be impartial as they edit, or programme, according to the tradition of the heterosexual consensus. Had things been otherwise, I personally might have been helped, during my mute years after leaving *The Times*, by encouragement to find a voice.

Meanwhile, heterosexual journalists tried to persuade me, in 1973, to make serious applications to the *Guardian*. I couldn't bring myself to – it was for financial journalistic work. I deliberately blew the interview. In 1974, desperate for money, I applied to the financial editor of the *Sunday Telegraph*. He said, yes, for his part, but he must refer it to the proprietor. The proprietor (Lord Hartwell) sent down word, I'm told, that a publicly-acknowledged homosexual should not be employed. I thought that an honest position on his part.

Now, as I write, I am that person I felt I couldn't possibly be, back in 1972. I am Editor of *Gay News*. It's an extraordinary feeling. An initiative I took so long ago on behalf of gays much less well informed, and mostly less privileged, than myself, had been sustained by others and nurtured into celebrity. It could now afford to pay me a wage. I could learn what it's like to fulfil the obligations of mainstream journalism (deadlines, accuracy, avoidance of libel, teamwork) in an entire company of out gays – to write for a 50,000 readership, virtually all of them gay, who would take for granted, and rightly, that they were reading the work of homosexuals. Out of the frying pan into the fire: from the moment of starting to write amongst others on *Gay News*, I have found a new limitation pressing as hardly on me as the old ones used to. Certainly I can be myself as I never once was in the years when I was employed by Fleet Street. It is the readership which now causes me difficulties; a restlessness makes me fantasise yet another kind of periodical. A quarterly, perhaps – something which would be launched and whose aims would be set by homosexuals, but which would seek to be read by, and to commission work from, heterosexuals fully as much as by homosexuals. Our perception would lead the way, but would not dictate the orientation of reader or writer or artist. As Editor of *Gay News* I have written one article each for the *Daily Express* and the *New Statesman*. But I have never yet written for a general audience in my own persona of out gay, on any topic that took my fancy. I have never been asked to.

An ungrateful restlessness, the future of *Gay News* being obscure and dark at the very instant I say these things. I only have to imagine the disappearance of the space it provides each fortnight to go cold; to remember the 1960s, when the El Vino mentality, the obeisance to cultural male heterosexuality, dominated all the media without a chink of light for the hundreds of thousands who want to read of (or see or listen to) other things besides; and without a chink of light for those whose abilities, like those of my lesbian and gay male colleagues on the various gay papers in the UK, could only be stifled into unrecognisable, closeted, compromise – or just utterly destroyed – if there were no one to accept or commission work except those who run even the supposedly liberal media of the 1980s. But as I say, you have to feel this truth to know it. In television studios, in radio stations, in groups of the heterosexually-oriented, and even in conversation with many a gay who's at ease with his world, I find resistance and even anger, when I put it forward. Those who wouldn't hesitate, in print or on the air, to refer to their possession of a husband or a wife or children, or to make one of the thousand oblique references to personal heterosexuality which I read or hear every day, protest against the intrusion of personal sexuality and private life into the media if homosexuals were to be out. I draw this much comfort from the resistance, and the bursts of irritation: only the arrival of a new idea could cause so much discomfort.

Chapter 14

STRANGE PLACES

Jill Tweedie

It is always darkest before the dawn they say and so do I. It was very damn dark in the mid-1930s when I was born and biology was destiny with a vengeance. Luckily for me, perhaps, that same destiny forced me to write or, rather, continue to write. I had turned out my first epic exercise-book novel at the age of eight and had gone on pouring forth poems and stories through marriage and the birth of two children, sustained in rejection by my husband's income and the help of an au pair. If my marriage had been happy, I might have made it as a novelist or I might have given up, discouraged, and become a proper housewife. As it was, divorce loomed and I became the breadwinner. Writing was the only hope I had to earn a living and look after children as well and writing had to take the form of journalism. Not for me the Shangri-la of fiction. The rewards, if any, would have been too little and too late, the bailiffs were at the door. That is no fancy imagery, either. Two large bailiffs, they were, who visited frequently and smiled like grand pianos, the only really reliable men in my life. They told me what they were going to do and they did it, woe was me.

So journalism was my economic lifeline. It turned out to be my psychic lifeline also. My anger at the way things were was given a more acceptable outlet than shop-lifting and shouting in the street and, two years after I started, the advent of organised feminism channelled individual angst into the universal. Feminist ideas were immensely exciting, they gave substance to what I knew in my bones and made me, like many other women, feel less crazy. They also explained my unease with the conventional masculine format of journalism, in which The Reporter got The Facts

and wrote up The Story, convinced that he was telling the
whole truth and nothing but the truth because it never
entered his head that he or his patriarchy might be funda-
mentally askew. Subjectivity was given a veneer of objectivity and, by keeping himself and his views concealed,
personal bias took on the weight of holy writ.

For all the excitement of those early days, though,
getting feminist ideas across in a national newspaper soon
became an uphill battle and one that was made no easier by
feminists' blanket dislike of the media (which I mostly
shared) and the media's blanket dislike of feminism. I was
trapped between the irresistible force and the apparently
immovable object, often counted a traitor by both sides, a
very flattening experience. I could do no right and the irony
was that I could not opt out, as I was often tempted to, because
I was a woman whose only expertise was women.

My great good fortune was that then, in 1969, I worked
for the *Guardian*, the only newspaper in Britain then that
tolerated feminist debate upon its pages. Naturally enough
I appreciated this, yet my very appreciation increased the
conflict between my outlook and that of entrenched anti-
media feminists. I knew how much my paper was risking
by even hesitantly championing a vastly unpopular cause
in the competitive climate of Fleet Street. The feminists
did not, it was not their business to care and in those first
few heady years they tarred every newspaper and every
journalist with the same brush, wielded with a fine disregard
for shades of grey, and who can blame them, seeing how
brutally they had been tarred and feathered for so long? Yet
I, for one, knew from the many letters I got that there
were women out there who were unlikely to be reached in
any other way than through a national newspaper and
through a personal column on a women's page. Arguments
abounded. The anti-media feminists loathed the very idea
of women's pages (so did we all at times) but we had to live
with the inexorable logistics of the paper's viability and
they did not. They were pure and we were compromised,
lackeys of the capitalist patriarchal Press. Worse, we did not
always appear to bear our burden of shame in a properly
humble manner! At the same time, like other feminist

journalists, I had my own battles to fight with male colleagues, unreconstructed chauvinists themselves at the time, who were none too enamoured of the issues raised and occasionally downright hostile, yet who were, for the most part, men of goodwill whose other concerns I shared. Confusion often reigned, a confusion that afflicted many other women in many other contexts but was made, I think, a fraction harder for those of my profession by our enforced isolation from feminist support, an isolation whose consequences are still visible in some media women who, transfixed in a time warp, pass on their fear of feminism to their readers to this day.

My own sustenance then and over the next ten years was the disembodied voice of the reader, the woman out there rather than the feminists I met and interviewed and talked to. Readers, I felt, were encumbered with difficulties far more recognisably my own than those that plagued the theorists of the movement, whose contributions were invaluable, invigorating but untried. In one sense, they were the officers and we were the foot soldiers slogging through mud, they gave the orders, we tried to carry them out and often failed, hung about as we were with delinquent husbands and intractable children collected in the unenlightened past, who unaccountably refused to respond to theories. I always relished the company of feminists for the euphoria of shared ideas but I felt real down-home solidarity with readers, they were the 'we' of me. That odd split, that mild schizophrenia, may, for all I know, reveal more about my individual temperament than my general situation and more about writers than women, since writers are usually quislings of a sort, Greeks smuggling themselves into Troy, wanting to be where they're not wanted, not wanting to be where they're wanted, true to themselves perhaps but only co-incidentally true to others.

Two years ago, my schizophrenic self came out of the closet with the fictional column 'Letters from a Faint-Hearted Feminist'. I began it partly to reassure the women who complained to me that they felt rejected by feminists because they were conventional housewives and mothers and partly for my own therapy. I have often imagined myself a

Mary, the radical separatist brave enough to reject the comforts of conformity, but I am always Martha, whose efforts to put theory into practice are so frequently thwarted by the incipient chaos of reality. Some admirable souls are able to banish all other commitments, loosen all other ties in favour of one over-riding concern to which they devote themselves with extraordinary tenacity. The rest of us have our times of courage and rebellion against the status quo but we are also doomed to face our weaknesses, exist with our contradictions and hold onto our sanity, usually by admitting our dashed hopes to each other and having a laugh. Women today are particularly vulnerable, damned if we don't and damned if we do by one faction or another, a no-win situation. Such ambivalences do not lend themselves to straight journalism or to polemic, only fiction offers room to manoeuvre without the hint of a lecture. Fiction also allows for the vagaries of life, the loose strands that refuse the tidying hand, the non sequiturs, the unanswerable questions, the questionable answers, the sheer disorder of things, in a way that journalism does not permit, dealing as it does with beginnings, middles and ends in a random world that has no perceptible beginning or middle, only the looming shadow of an end.

Predictably, Martha and her letters have drawn flak from some feminists and understandably so. It would be nice to believe that women no longer fell into the feminine trap or lived out feminine clichés, that we could all change fuses and tyres, hold down demanding jobs while suckling infants, break with the family or eat recalcitrant husbands and sons for breakfast. It would be even nicer to believe that if writers refused to portray what is called 'the stereotype', it would simply go away. But we can't and it won't. More to the point, uplifting Soviet-Realist-type images of women can sometimes be severely counter-productive. That they are necessary is beyond argument but there is another need – to avoid making us feel failures by comparison and, because of that, hostile to the image and to the women who manage to live up to it. If you can persuade women who have little confidence in themselves (and who amongst us has much more?) that falling by the wayside does not signify the end of the journey, is that not worth doing? Our daughters must have trail-blazing women to admire and emulate but they must also learn to live with messy, peculiar, often incompetent, loving human beings who try and fail and try again. And some of these will continue to be women.

Now I am writing a novel, having put myself in training for the long-distance haul with an earlier non-fiction book. There are amazing women who cope with children while producing books but, sadly, I am not one of them. My own writing efforts exactly mirror my various phases of motherhood. In my twenties and thirties, young children fragmented my attention span so much that I could only produce in short 2000-word sprints, paid for immediately to bail out my always perilously low financial boat. My first book, the non-fiction *In The Name of Love*, coincided with a healthier bank account and the last child's arrival at the age of puberty and growing independence, giving me the chance to settle at my desk for longer periods and flex the flabby muscles of my concentration. With this novel, the last child is nearly a man and I can afford to gamble at last. Besides, what better way to mark the Change of Life than by changing that life?

Fiction has done that, all right. I was weary for the moment of the constrictions of journalism and tired of writing about women within them. The high fever of feminist ideas had passed; in the 1980s they need grounding in the nitty-gritty of economics, trade unionism, political action, the legal system, the hard graft of practice and participation and the marshalling of facts. Vital work but not for me and I am old enough to say so without too many apologies, suffering as I presently am from acute feminist indigestion, a state that exactly parallels ordinary indigestion: an over-indulgence in good food causing temporary but painful heartburn and a need to avert the mind from the cause until appetite returns.

Nevertheless, my novel deals with four women who are manipulated by men and by a male world at various levels from the emotional to the political. I have made a conscious effort to write about the outer rather than the inner world because I myself can no longer read books by women about their search for themselves after divorce and such intimate matters. I am constantly astonished and awed by how well so many women write, but these conventional subjects, however important, bore me now. I feel an urgent need to move out of the claustrophobic recesses of the heart and the hearth and into the wide, cold, wicked spaces where men play power games that are likely to finish us all before we are half-way along the road to sexual equality or any other kind. I do not feel up to the task I have set myself and am quite resigned to the knowledge that I have aimed well above the level of my competence, but there are rewards in trying.

And writing fiction has certainly changed me. I am still sure of absolute wrong but much less certain of absolute right. My judgments of my fellow human beings have radically altered, too. Until now, I tended to measure people according to my view of their 'worth', their 'morality' and other distinctly pious and puritan criteria. Now, I revel in the marvellous diversity of human character, I delight in its unpredictability and its eccentricities, I am fascinated by the whole rather than the parts. As a journalist I was interested in what people said, as a budding novelist I am more interested in the way they say it, the infinite nuances of expression that reveal or conceal. I have been invaded by amorality, I have worked up an omniverous appetite for both good and evil, I want to stare at the machinery and watch it work, suspending all judgment for the pleasures of the feast.

It is a curious and bewildering reversal that often shocks the familiar part of me, that more principled indignant self that is fast vanishing under a deluge of impressions. The complexities of human behaviour and emotion absorb me far more now than my former simplistic approach – are you for us or against us, one of Us or one of Them? The multi-shaded greys of life have taken over from the sharp blacks and whites, infinite layers are burying the concrete mass, I am detached and yet wholly conversant with the evils I see all around me, never more so. I cannot explain or justify this sea-change except in its connection with writing fiction. I am in no position to decide if my outlook now is 'better' or 'worse' though I watch it carefully for symptoms of corruption. Is this giving up or moving on? I do not know. Still, it is a strange place I find myself in and I like strange places.

Chapter 15

TWO STEPS FORWARD, ONE STEP BACK?

Angela Phillips

When Michelene asked me to contribute to this book she said that the different areas of my life – politics, writing, trades unionism, and parenthood – seemed remarkably unified. But it doesn't feel unified to me. Most of my energy seems to be spent in servicing all the different fragments just to stop the fabric dropping apart altogether. Sometimes I feel that, if I could only chop a bit off, the rest would have an opportunity to thrive, but each bit seems to be dependent on the next. Maybe that is a kind of unity.

I had just returned from a union conference when I received Michelene's letter. The effort of combining mother-hood and trades unionism with politics and work had left me feeling worn out, fed up and left out. Consciousness is rising in trade unions but so far only as far as providing a crèche. Once the working day had finished, childcare was once more an individual responsibility. It's no fun spending your evenings alone with a sleeping child when the rest of your colleagues are drinking, talking, plotting and organising for tomorrow.

It was having a baby which tipped the balance of my life from high-speed chaos to near disintegration. It brought home to me with real force the hopelessly unbalanced nature of a society which is organised solely for the needs of people without responsibility for children. As a journalist and a trades unionist, I am constantly forced to make excuses and ask favours of a childless society. As a feminist I am enraged by the lack of sympathy and support offered even by those who profess to understand the problem. And, as a mother, I feel that I should redouble my efforts to fight for political changes. The only trouble is, I'm too tired.

It was anger which led me into journalism in the first place. If I had previously experienced anything which could be described as an ambition it was to be a fashion photographer. But that was Before Feminism. For me, discovering the Women's Liberation Movement was like cleaning a thick layer of dirt off the window through which I looked at life. For the first time, the world made sense. No longer were the frustrations of being female simply a set of random happenings, affecting only me, there was a reason for it all.

It would be hard to express, even to today's feminists, just what sisterhood meant in the early 1970s. It was like falling in love. In fact for many women, it was falling in love. The love affair was sadly brief but it provided an atmosphere of total trust in which to learn how to think and how to act. I had been trained as a photographer but soon I found photographs inadequate as a means of expression. There was just too much to say.

So I learned to write. First in the *Women's Report* collective where better educated women laughed at my spelling and explained the meaning of new words and concepts. Then on *Spare Rib*, its politics unformed, its direction uncertain but its commitment, to the inexperienced, total. Within the movement these publications have a vital purpose but they don't reach very far outside the circle of the committed and I wanted to move beyond that circle.

No one is outside the reach of radical ideas, but few people are in the right place at the right time and with the appropriate intellectual tools, so ideas pass us by. For me, an important part of political action is to find ways of passing messages across to those women whose minds have been imprisoned by male ideas of their place, their interests and their abilities.

The contrast between those early experiences with the alternative press, and the world of the mass media was immense. It took a lot of courage to pick up a phone and suggest a story to a 'real' editor and it was years before I could walk into a newspaper office without coming out in a cold sweat. But I was lucky. In those buoyant days before the recession bit hard, there was some room for liberalism and experiment. The women's movement was news, and I was part of it, so doors opened.

Despite its interest in fashion and fads, the British media represents only the narrowest band of opinion. It is owned and controlled by a small number of men who, while they may not interfere directly in day-to-day editorial decisions, make sure that those in charge are on their side. There is one area which has tended to lie outside their sphere of interest: women. As far as the proprietors are concerned, women make useful readers only as consumers, who bring in advertising.

While political bias keeps the general news coverage running along the narrow tracks of the political centre, the need to encourage advertising has always taken the sting out of Women's Pages and magazines even as consumer watchdogs. However, until recently, the possibility that women's interests could be political had simply not occurred to those in control. It was this paternalistic lack of interest that allowed feminism to creep into the press in the mid 1970s, and one of the places where it was allowed to settle and flourish was the *Guardian* women's page. There is no evidence to suggest that this was deliberate editorial policy. It just proved impossible to recruit a good editor who did not learn to identify, to some degree with feminist ideas. Indeed it would be hard for a woman whose mind was not closed to fight for survival in the male world of newspapers and remain entirely untouched by the only analysis which makes sense of that struggle.

Working for the *Guardian* was still not without its contradictions. Although for the best part of six years, I barely had a single idea turned down, I always felt like an outsider. I provided a service with the minimum of social exchange. So I was amazed when, in the spring of 1979, the then editor of the Women's Page, Liz Forgan, asked me to contribute a column of Women's Movement news.

The idea was both challenging and alarming. A column written from a feminist point of view would label me forever and make it very difficult to contribute general features for the page. On the other hand, how could I turn down an opportunity to provide direct access for the movement to thousands of women every fortnight?

One way out would have been to provide a politically neutral news digest, self-censored and safe, a solution which I would have found hard to live with. In a way the problem was taken out of my hands. I decided that it would be wrong to make personal use of my access to news via *Spare Rib*, where I worked once a week. So I arranged to share the column with Jill Nicholls (who at that time co-ordinated the *Spare Rib* news pages). Without Jill's involvement, I doubt that I could have resisted the urge to play safe and protect myself.

Taking the copy in every fortnight was always a nerve-racking business. We were often asked to justify our stories and we spent far more time on the column than the meagre payment could possibly have justified on any commercial basis. After the first column Liz Forgan told us that our copy would never be allowed near the prime position at the top of the page, and its length was cut back. We were expected to cover three separate topics, all fresh, original stories, but we were paid the same rate as we would have got for a short single issue feature.

It was difficult to find the right voice to speak in. Were we reporting news according to the accepted rules – allowing the facts to speak for themselves – or were we expressing opinion? It was never quite clear. Where our comments conformed with acceptable opinion they were left untouched. When they moved into the dangerous area of radical feminism they caused discomfort. One subject which really offended was menstruation. As far as I remember, the only story that they ever cut out was about deodorised Playtex tampons, a subject which shortly afterwards became a matter of national attention and the subject of a whole page of features in the *Guardian*.

When, after eighteen months, the column was cut, the main reason we were given was that it contained insufficient original material and too much opinion. The letter came at the end of August, a period when, as every news reporter knows, very little happens. Judging by the number of our stories which were re-hashed in various parts of the paper in the ensuing months, we can't have been doing too badly for new material. In any case the suddenness of the decision belies the reasoning. No attempt was made to change our direction, our content or our style. It's hard to believe that the decision was anything other than political.

Although Liz Forgan assured us that the end of the column didn't mean the end of us as *Guardian* contributors, we both turned our attention to drumming up work in other neglected areas. In fact, my name only appeared on the page once more before Liz was replaced by an editor who at last fulfilled the long sought-after role of a bulwark against radicalism. It has not appeared again since.

Of course I am not the only writer who has suffered this fate. Although occasional feminist contributions do surface on the page, they are rarely by professional writers. With the exception of Jill Tweedie the *Guardian* now uses very few experienced journalists who have any personal understanding of feminism.

Jill Tweedie has said of the *Guardian*'s recruitment process for women's editor: 'There's hundreds and thousands of books, papers and pages of research written about women, but they don't care about that. They think the only qualification you need is to be a woman. It's like saying that, because he's toting a gun on his hip, a man can be defence correspondent.' Exactly the same line of reasoning seems to be employed in the choice of writers for the page.

Sadly, the patriarchal takeover of the women's page in the only national daily newspaper which was open to progressive ideas, has been allowed to happen with very little protest. Many feminists were so used to castigating the *Guardian* for its middle-class trendiness that they haven't stopped to analyse what has been lost. Where are the voices defending the gains that have been made over the last few years? We have lost our only voice, and we haven't even noticed.

While the voice of independent feminism is being quietly stifled in newspapers, it is worming its way back into print through the women's magazine market. Newspaper journalists have always rather looked down on their colleagues in magazines but really this is a much maligned and undervalued area. Of course, with their three-month time gaps between writing and publication, they lack the power of the daily press to influence current events as they happen. But that power is useless if the people are not listening.

Women do, of course, read newspapers, but as they are so self-evidently written largely by and for men, there are few points with which female readers can easily identify. News is written according to a set of news values which, with some exceptions, headlines those matters over which ordinary people feel they have least influence. Magazines present life in a very different way and at a pace which is closer to the rhythm of people's lives. To be sure, much of what makes up the average woman's magazine is pure escapist nonsense, but among the eulogies about royalty and the stars, a new form of magazine journalism is emerging.

Woman's Own and *Honey*, working for two entirely different groups of readers, have done much to break down the advertisers' stereotypes of what women will read. *Woman's Own* has focussed readers' attention on issues which affect them, such as childcare and equal opportunities, via well publicised readership surveys. *Honey* has developed an idiosyncratic style which successfully mixes fashion and fun with quite radical feminism.

For me, the greatest joy of working for women's magazines is the fact that you are likely to be working with editors who do not see feminist ideas as a threat, either to their positions or their readers. Gradually, young women who were exposed to feminism at university are working their way up the hierarchies to a position where they can, cautiously, express their own views. They see most of the central issues of the movement as quite legitimate areas of public debate. Some feminists see this 'normalising' of radical thought as a threat. Such purism is not for me. I do not care in the least whether a woman discovers that a hankering for independence is normal through the pages of *Woman's Own* or *Spare Rib*.

These editors are able to express their feelings about women because they are not so directly controlled by men as are the women who work for newspapers. Hard-hitting articles about abortion, sexual violence and pornography now appear regularly in magazines. Yet I know of one recent occasion, when a long article on violence against women was removed at page setting stage by the editor of a national newspaper because it seemed anti-men. On another occasion, the editor of a newspaper objected to a personal account of a rape experience printed, with perfect timing, at the start of a national media debate on the subject of rape and sentencing policy. I was once told that an article on vaginal infections couldn't be printed in a national Sunday tabloid because it might offend the readers.

In the cosy ghetto of women's magazines, practically nothing is taboo any more but that doesn't mean that there are no rules. An article printed virtually without changes in *Honey* or *Cosmopolitan* would be totally re-written in *Woman* or *Woman's Own*. The mass circulation weeklies take their responsibility to the readers extremely seriously. Unfortunately that often extends to protecting them from new ideas. Everything is checked and rechecked and then re-written until it becomes bland and uncontroversial.

Working for a magazine which slaughters your copy is demoralising. I sometimes wonder whether it is worth trying to get the message across when it gets so badly mangled on the way. Nevertheless, the answer must still be 'yes'. Wherever feminist writers have got a toe in the door of the mass media, they have got to keep it there. During the next few years, the ideological battle to return women to house-bound dependence on men will hot up. We no longer have a front-line position to fight from so we will have to manage by passing our messages behind the lines of men who will no doubt attempt to debate our future for us.

Chapter 16

WOMEN IN NEWSPAPERS

Mary Stott

It sounded easy to write about women and newspapers. I have been writing for newspapers for more than half a century. My mother started contributing to a little local newspaper founded and edited by my father and printed by my grandfather before she was married in 1900. But when I started to think about newspapers in *relation* to women both as readers and as journalists, I realised there were a great many tangled threads to try to straighten out. For instance, if Harriet Martineau would write regular leaders for the *Daily News* in the mid-nineteenth century, why do so few women contribute leaders to national newspapers today, when the profession is supposed to have been opened up to them? In the fifteen years I edited the women's page of the *Guardian* and came to be quite knowledgeable about women's affairs, no one ever suggested I should write a leader on any subject whatsoever. Women *are* asked to write leaders on their special subjects today, but I doubt if any woman is a regular member of any leader-writing team on any serious newspaper.

Another interesting puzzle: why has it never been possible to run a successful newspaper by women for women? In the last few years I have been contacted by many good feminists convinced that there was a substantial readership for a weekly, if not daily, newspaper for women which would reflect our interests and be our mouthpiece. So far as I know, none has succeeded, and alas I never had any real faith that they would. It is forgotten now that even the greatest of newspaper tycoons, Lord Northcliffe, failed in an enterprise of this kind. I have known for years that the *Daily Mirror* started life as a paper for women, but only recently have I learned the details of this remarkable enterprise, from a fascinating essay in the *Journalism Studies Review* of the Centre for Journalism Studies at University College, Cardiff.

The author, Jeffrey Wright, asserts that in 1893 Lady Florence Dixie was planning a halfpenny daily for women; that George Newnes, creator of *Titbits*, was planning a specific appeal to women readers in his *Daily Courier*; and that there were persistent rumours in Fleet Street that the Suffragette Women's International Progressive Union was conducting negotiations about a newspaper with the famous journalist W. T. Stead. (If this name is correct, it disproves the contention of many historians of the women's movement that it was the *Daily Mail* that coined the name 'suffragettes' after the Pankhursts' militant campaign opened in 1905 – as, indeed, they coined the term 'flapper voter' for the women who went to the polls at the age of twenty-one for the first time in 1929 – who included me.)

Northcliffe launched his *Daily Mirror*, a paper for gentlewomen by gentlewomen, on 3 November 1903, less than a month after the formation of the WSPU. It was edited by Mrs Mary Howarth, until then women's editor of the *Daily Mail*, with an all-female staff. Northcliffe thought he had a great success on his hands but he was wrong. The first print of 276,000 dropped to 143,000 on the second day, and had fallen to 100,000 within a week. Two months after its launch, Northcliffe turned the paper into the *Daily Illustrated Mirror*, for both men and women – the true ancestor of today's tabloids. Women didn't want their own paper then. I doubt if they want their own paper now.

Poor Mary Howarth was obviously a flop, but if Northcliffe thought her good enough to try her out as editor of a national newspaper in 1903, why has no newspaper proprietor since thought it worth while to try a woman in the chair? There are women of top quality and vast experience of helping to run the show in Fleet Street today, like Felicity Green, formerly of the *Mirror* now of the *Express*, yet when any newspaper (or indeed, any women's magazine) flags and falters, the owners always send for yet another man. It must be at least a dozen years since I said at a luncheon party in the House of Commons: 'I think there could be a woman Prime Minister before there is a woman editing a Fleet Street newspaper.' Little did I think then how soon we were to see Margaret Thatcher's triumphant arrival in Downing Street, while the Fleet Street women are still waiting in the wings.

Another newspaper riddle: Why does the women's page persist in these egalitarian times, even though it is less often labelled in any way as 'for women'? My mother ran a 'Mainly for Women' column in the *Leicester Mercury* in the 1920s. I ran a Mainly for Women page in the *Guardian* from 1957 to 1972. I was only nineteen when I was assigned to women's page journalism on the *Leicester Mail* and bitterly I grieved over it. I thought that becoming 'Lestrienne' (imagine it!) was the end of me as a 'real' journalist and I was pretty well right. Only for five years, at the end of the Second World War, did I truly escape from women's journalism into the genderless world of an evening newspaper's sub-editors' room.

I said bitterly when this blow fell in 1926, 'The women's page is an anachronism. Newspapers don't need it any more. Women don't need it.' So I listen sardonically when young people of both sexes say at seminars and conferences, as if they were making an astonishing new discovery, 'Why a women's page now? Why not a special page for men?' There is, of course, an important commercial reason why the women's page persists. Women are still reckoned to be the shoppers. Advertisements for all kinds of consumer goods, from clothes and cosmetics to kitchen appliances and furniture, food, and even drink, are thought likely to have the best chance of attracting purchasers if they are placed on the women's page. But readers may like to reflect on the fact that the women's page which is most strongly feminist-oriented, the *Guardian's*, has the fewest consumer display ads. (I personally think that the criterion for judging whether a women's page advertisement will 'pull' is not how much fashion, cookery and consumer guidance it contains, but how avidly it is read. Even the most Liberationist Mum buys disposable nappies and baby powder, doesn't she?)

A change is discernible in the naming, content and appearance of 'women's' pages in the serious newspapers. The most notable gender labels are now 'Guardian Women' and 'Femail'. The *Daily* and *Sunday Telegraph* have no label at all. *The Times* does not separate features addressed mainly to women from general features. The *Observer* ran through 'Ego', 'Hers', 'You' (imagine answering a telephone query 'Who is that, please?' with the monosyllable 'You'), and 'Living', before settling on 'Sunday Plus'. The *Sunday Times* has been faithful to 'Look'. The trend obviously is towards recognising that there is a good deal on a well-edited women's page which appeals to men as well as women and that they should not be put off by being observed to read a page plainly labelled as female. *Guardian* men clearly are not.

When in 1963 the *Guardian* opened up discussion of whether the label 'Mainly for Women' should be changed, I had a letter which was such a perfect example of blinkered masculinity that I have treasured it ever since. It ran: 'Your contributor Mary Stott is apt to overlook that the *Guardian* is a *man's* paper and that the women's page is usually passed over to women by men after they have judged it important enough to do so. The whole tone, temper and subject of the paper is insufficiently ephemeral to be widely known to women. For the foregoing reasons it seems to me immaterial whether to change the name or not.' I would delight to quote the full name of the author of this delicious letter from Long Melford, Suffolk, but perhaps by now his wife or his daughter has re-educated him, so I will only say, 'God bless you, Mr R. B. H. B.'

There are other reasons than ad appeal for continuing to have a page for women in serious papers, whatever it is called, even in the 1980s. Having our own space, our own standard of judgment about how that space should be used, meant, in my time as a women's page editor, that the readers, of whom many in the 1960s were feeling their way towards a new kind of spiritual independence, could put forward their own creative ideas about society. Out of that ferment of ideas came, for example, the Pre-School Playgroups Association, the National Association for the Welfare of Children in Hospital, the Disablement Incomes Group, the National Council for the Single Woman and her Dependents, the Association for the Improvement of the Maternity Services and many others – including the National Housewives

Register. This is by no means a consumer-oriented collection of homebodies, but a remarkably efficient organisation of 25,000 or so young women who, while choosing to be at home during their children's early childhood, want to keep their minds alert and well-informed.

Women's pages have undoubtedly grown more prestigious in the last few years. Men are now really very pleased to be asked to contribute (and of course, to edit them. It is a common assumption among male journalists that they know at least as well as and probably better than women journalists what women readers want!). More than that, a woman does not lose status or the opportunity to move into other forms of newspaper work by moving into what I used to call 'the female ghetto'. One *Guardian* women's page editor came from a London evening newspaper for which she wrote leaders and moved on to TV's Channel Four. Another moved across from being economics editor. Such changes are likely to be more common now that women have distinguished themselves in so many specialties – not just health and welfare, education, social services, housing and similar subjects always thought to appeal to women, but in finance and investment, politics, sport and even defence. There have been several women war correspondents, including the legendary Clare Hollingworth who seemed to her male colleagues totally without physical fear.

These special correspondents indicate progress of a substantial kind for newspaper women. They are important as role models for younger women and they have the opportunity to influence readers' thinking on social and political issues – not that the influence of newspapers can be reckoned as great now as the influence of TV. Probably the days of the mass circulation newspaper are already numbered. Leading columnists and diarists know full well that they are better known for what they say on the Box than what they write in their newspapers.

Yet newspapers, especially the serious ones, do still have a great attraction for women of quality. What seems curious and saddening to me is that so few of the people who actually *make* the paper, the editor, night editor, managing editor, chief sub-editor, news editor, features editor, are women.

When you read of great newspapers like *The Times* or the *Observer* being bought and sold, do you ever read of a *woman* being involved at board or executive level in the negotiations? Does any newspaper owned by a Trust, like the *Observer* or the *Guardian*, have a woman trustee? I doubt it.

To some extent women should blame themselves for their lack of progress towards the top executive jobs. It is natural, I suppose, that the glamour of the by-line should appeal so strongly to the sex who have suffered anonymity for so long. But editors are not drawn from writers, however brilliant. They come from the 'behind the scenes' men – what my husband used to call 'the back bench' – the journalists who really make the paper, decide what goes into it and how it shall be presented. Certainly not until there are far more women *in charge* of the news gathering and presentation processes, the direction and the policy-making shall we have much hope of eradicating sexist language – especially in headlines, which at present are *almost all* written by men, or derogatory images of women in public and private life. The classic example, quoted in the National Union of Journalists' guidelines for promoting equality through journalism, is a *Daily Mirror* headline to a parliamentary report, 'Redhead took on a honey-blonde yesterday' – the redhead being Barbara Castle and the honey-blonde Margaret Thatcher. The pressure group 'Women in Media' was formed partly to combat offensive rubbish of that kind, and since it was formed, in 1970, by dedicated members of the new women's movement, there has undoubtedly been *some* progress. No longer are intelligent, conscientious journalists on the serious papers quite so ready to mock women's activities.

Newspaper writing can, as C. P. Scott declared, be as good as any writing in the world, and far removed from utilitarian hackwork. Time and space are the journalist's masters, and they inexorably demand both clarity and brevity. Only in columns and personal comment should the sex of the writer reveal itself, for skill and craftsmanship have no gender, whether in writing or in making pots or cooking. But the skill needed to convey a complicated series of events or a complicated thought so clearly that it will hold the reader's attention and comprehension from first to last is of a high order, and it certainly has never been confined to men!

Chapter 17

ON THE EDGE

Irving Weinman

I'm trying to write about an edge, the boundary between my sexism and my pro-feminism, though the latter's a term I learned only lately, sign of how geological the process is, I mean feminism a tide against the rocks of my assumptions. To start with a recent example: watching a Chabrol film on the telly with the woman I live with and a friend, a feminist in her early twenties. *The Butcher*, it's called, a film I remember liking when first seen about ten years back. Story of a woman teacher in a small provincial town who becomes friendly with a man she begins to suspect, correctly, of committing a series of grisly murders of women and girls. About two-thirds of the way into it, the younger woman friend is bored or angry; she turns away from the screen. The film ends.

Me: Well, didn't you like it?

Younger Woman: No. Awful, vicious sexism. It just makes me sick.

Me: But she's sympathetic. I mean, she doesn't succumb to him. He kills himself rather than harm her.

Younger Woman: No. Beneath the pretty pictures it's the same old disgusting message: had she slept with the butcher he wouldn't have had to kill. In other words, the woman is somehow responsible for the murders and even for his suicide!

Me: (pause) Yes. Jesus, you're right. Just shows I'm not such a hot feminist.

Younger Woman: Feminist? You're not a feminist. You can't be – you're a man. Pro-feminist maybe, but not a feminist.

The point is I didn't see it; the point is it took a woman to

133

show it to me; here I still was regarding myself as a feminist and proud of it when it was just another typical male appropriation of language no less stupidly defensive than as a white man imagining myself a black radical. Also my own version of the film's sub-text, because I went on to tell this friend that women should beware us appropriators; in other words, the real point, I neatly turned my problem into a women's problem.

Feminism, like Marxism some years before, first came to me intellectually. Mid to late 1960s. Friedan, Greer, those first books (later and so much more powerfully Adrienne Rich's *Of Woman Born* read with rage and tears like I sat reading on an electric chair of self-recognition as the bad guy; but that, as I say, was later). Up to then in my writing the usual unconscious sexism; women in my poetry written from the hegemony of male assumption that shames me now, didn't then, some of it then even published in liberal-lefty little mags no more, I guess, than one-third funded by the CIA, or maybe that's just a metaphor of my head's sexist infiltration.

But in the beginning of some change, I know it involved the kids, having a daughter and a son and seeing my attitudes bounced back at me out of them and not much liking what I saw and so damned undeniable as opposed to the glib objectivity of reading. No question of my yakking attitudes, those kids reflected what I was. So it began to come to me, slowly, that things I wanted different for my daughter couldn't be different for her, and for my son of course, without being different for all women, and all men of course. This is so obvious after the fact but not then. Like the try at my own consciousness.

This is me, late 1960s, talking a pretty good imitation of feminist line, living it differently, fighting it tooth and nail: 'Go out and do something, get involved in women's liberation,' I commanded my wife.

Now I see that part of it must have been the women's movement, tide beneath the thick man bulwarks of self image, that brought me into analysis, early mid 1970s. My analyst a woman, very calm, very quiet, and a geiger counter to my radioactive bullshit. Me? Me hate women? Oh, no, man,

I loved women, really. Really? Twice a week for two years' deconstruction, falling walls, the armour clanking off. And only as I started to see how I hated women could anything positive begin to build. The old analysis preceding synthesis.

Well, for one thing, I could start to *read* my old writing. A typical bit:

> We sail at daybreak to be drowned:
> Calypso was too good to us –
> we need some whores to steer our course.

(1966)

You get it? how I loved women?

And my starting to get it produced something important for my writing. (Setting it down like this makes it more linear/rational than it could have been, but it's something like this.) Finding how received my attitudes towards women were made me consider the entire stance and language and rhythm of my poetry. How unreal I could then see the whole thing was. It made me consider how bizarrely locked into my poetry past I still was. In the late 1950s I'd been part of that 'famous' Robert Lowell poetry seminar in the States; the master himself and Anne Sexton and Sylvia Plath and that whole confessional movement. Now, I'm not here going to argue whether Plath and/or Sexton were or were not proto-feminists, but what I took from them, what *I* made out of it was something like cheap irony, an easy anguish that not only demeaned my subjects but kept me from finding my own voice in poetry. And as long as I remained this vampire, my poetry would be anaemic.

Yet this is distorted, because to claim this awareness as coming mostly or directly from my relation to feminism would be to omit other real sources: socialism, literature, other arts, the daily business of being a husband, father, son, brother, friend of other people, lecturer, commuter, consumer and sexual human.

Moreover, my relation to feminism has to be put in its social context, has no meaning outside that. Whatever stage of life, I'm someone very influenced by women, liking the company of women. Operative here is some cultural difference between me and many British men. I grew up in America, always in co-education; women were part of my daily work/play environment – and this has to make a big difference for my, and I'd guess any man's, social assumptions. Much of it, then, as simple as my being in everyday contact with women and more and more women in this period with a developing feminist consciousness. Given this background, I couldn't discount this feminist consciousness as belonging to some women 'out there' but had to confront it because it belonged to these women 'in here', a range of real people in my life.

So, OK, not the sole or primary cause, but feminism some way connected with beginning to write my own poetry. By 1977 in *Eye of the Storm* (published 1978, Many Press):

NONE here
but the sexless
rational witches that swirl
    at the fringe
    of language

    still more sensible
    to women
    kitchen conditioned utensil mad
        simple beeswax
        and the cooking pot

Two other sorts of contact with, if not feminism, women's consciousness, had special significance for me. Anne Sexton was a friend of mine; in 1974, two years after her death, I organised and helped devise a memorial evening for her in London, at the now defunct Little Theatre. I worked with Judith Kazantzis, Diana Scott and Valerie Sinason and learned more from their sometimes coinciding, sometimes divergent readings of Anne's poetry than I ever would have known on my own or from only male interpretations. More, these women began opening my eyes to a range of women's writing to which I'd been blind.

The second contact, also in the mid 1970s: because my wife was teaching basic reading skills to some of the kids at Chiswick Women's Aid whom the local schools couldn't (that is, wouldn't) cope with, I came into contact with battered women. This was, of course, disturbing and thought-provoking, but I knew I was such a gentle big guy – never even *thought* of hitting my wife or kids. So, after reading Erin Pizzey's *Scream Quietly* . . . I decided to write a music play loosely based on the lines of that book. At the time, I was interested in aspects of puppet theatre and decided to write the play in the mode of Punch and Judy, that classic of pure violence. Strange things happened to me writing that play, *Punch Judy Punch*, generally, things to do with confronting my own suppressed physical violence. Here I was consciously and intellectually dedicated to revealing the private and societal evils of battering, but emotionally something else was going on. It wasn't that I was enjoying the violence pouring from my pen, but obviously I'd opened some deep springs of violent fantasy – the violent bits were so much easier for me to write; it was so much easier to imagine (and write) what Punch was up to than to do the same for Judy. Scarey, but there it was: Punch was part of me and Judy wasn't; Punch developed in my writing, raged and smashed across the pages. I had to write and rewrite and rewrite Judy who still remained so flat a character, though I knew the *idea* was that this should be her play. It never was. Judy had all the right, but what good was that when Punch had all the life? Not that I literally became a batterer, but during those months working on the play I was jumpy and growling. With hindsight, I know I was out of my depth, out of control.

I think my male experience made it impossible for me to bring it off. Whether *the* male experience precludes bringing it off is a more complex question. True, there's Hardy's Tess, but the outrage done her is still, I think, revealed through essentially male writer projections: familial outrage through her father, class outrage through Alec D'Urbeville, the outrage of liberal idealism done through Angel, and all this against the socio-economic outrage of the (then) new rural capitalism affecting south-west England. There seem two pertinent conclusions. First, I believe that only a woman could successfully write the play I had in mind. Second, as a writer, I have to be aware of what sort of fantasies, what modes of my imagination, I'm touching on (touching off) and

make them work as best I can. And when they don't work or
work in the wrong way, I have to, as a political person, simply
scrap them. So I scrapped it; fifteen or even ten years ago, I
don't think I would have scrapped *Punch Judy Punch*.

Recently, goaded in the best possible way (which is to say
inspired) by the woman I live with, I've started writing prose
– short stories. Many of them are more or less auto-
biographically based workings of adolescent experience, and,
given mine, are about aspects of sexuality. But to narrate
from my present consciousness would distort them, since I
want to reveal not only the experience but the adolescent
male's *sense* of the experience, the meaning it has for him. So,
in some, the narrator is the adolescent male to whom the
story's happening. So, in some, the narrator's a few years
away from the action, able to tell the story with a bit more
objectivity but still not aware of what it is he can't or won't
understand (or why). And this means that the women, the
girls, in these stories are often another species of being;
attractive or repulsive, they're merely projections of
adolescent male homo-social rivalry.

Now, these ironies will be understood if I've written the
stories right. But it's risky. Because if I haven't written them
right, the reader, especially the aware woman reader, will
find them just crudely sexist. And, naturally, not writing
them right means my not being able to think/feel them right,
which is also the gauge of whatever sexism is really in me.
But how the hell can I try this without taking the risk? And I
can't believe I shouldn't try.

If this sounds sanctimonious, I don't intend it to be.
Understand: I certainly don't start writing these stories from
the question, 'Let's see, how can I bring an awareness of
patriarchal society out of these incidents?' No. But in writing
them, in remembering, imagining, recreating, I'm certainly
working with the consciousness I have, so there's always the
attempt at balancing the ironies while trying to make any
reader want to keep turning the pages. And what I learn from
male writer friends as well as from my reading is that what
I'm trying to do isn't in the mainstream of contemporary male
writing about sexuality.

First, as my agent keeps telling me, the short story just

isn't the popular form it was even, say, twenty years ago. Well, that, I guess, is my problem. But more to the point of this essay is my sense that in attempting to write stories in which certain ironies reveal the process by which the adolescent male incorporates patriarchal values, I'm trying something very different from the viewpoint of other male writers, today. I mean the *Portnoy's Complaint* viewpoint, in which the ostensible object of irony is the male character while the real butt of its sexual irony is the female. Or even with more 'sensitive' writers, with Pynchon or even Bellow, for instance, the ironies don't seem made to reveal the simple injustice of male objectifications of women. Yet, while I feel it's disingenuous of any male writer who pretends to an awareness of the problem saying he just writes his male characters 'the way they are' (since the writer not only 'recreates' a world, he creates a moral world), I admit that I don't suffer from a sense of isolation in this respect. For one thing, I'm too busy trying to do what I want; for another, it might be that other male writers are trying this and aren't bringing it off – the very problem I spoke of in defining what I'm trying to do, among other things, in my short stories.

And that problem is relatively simple compared to the problem of the stories in the next material stage of the process – the market. Because, needing to make some sort of living from my writing, what do I do when my agent figures I (which means the two of us) can best do this by trying to place those with most 'prurient interest' in those low, high-paying magazines? Never mind whose prurience – his, mine, the editor's, the average six-figure income a year young US male stockbroker-lawyer reader's. You know what I mean. Do I say no no, send it out to respectable little mags and try to eat my payment of three copies? Do I pretend that where they're published and who reads them is irrelevant to what the stories are, what material thing they are in this material world? And do I have an answer for these questions? Not offhand, not theoretically, I don't.

This is what feminism has meant to me, to my writing: not only more awareness of women as real people in the real world, but awareness of aspects of myself with which I wasn't in touch before. And this, I feel, means some possibilities of a broadening and deepening of subject and attitude towards subject in my writing. And this, too, full of risk: the risk of appropriation and complacency, the risk of feeling that I'm not sexist just because some other men are more sexist. Sexism, then, like racism, imperialism, other dehumanising 'isms' in me. And as a person who's a writer, all I can do is try to keep moving away out to that eroding edge. On that edge trying to hear the tide, risking that.

Chapter 18

THE DIALOGUE OF GENDER

Penelope Shuttle and Peter Redgrove

Michelene: Can you each say first, whether your gender is important to you when you write – in choice of subject matter (for poetry, non-fiction, novels) and/or in treatment – i.e. approach, choice of imagery.

Penelope and Peter: We can say jointly. Briefly, we see sexual differences, anatomy, giving preferential or privileged access to different gender experiences. Thus, because you are a woman, you are not debarred from masculine experiences or feelings; but by virtue of being a woman, you are clearly closer to experiencing feminine matters; it is your starting-point; you may want to diverge. We do see gender differences as being flexible, and the roles as being largely learnt; but we do also see an inclination towards different kinds of life-experience brought about by the two kinds of endowment, as man or woman. Thus, for example, a woman has *direct* access to the experiences we know as menstruation and the menstrual cycle. She also has direct access to the other sex-based thresholds in her life: menarche, conception, pregnancy, labour and parturition, lactation, menopause. These direct experiences are the basis of gender differences: a person can be more masculine or feminine according to how much he or she allows the experiences provided by the sex differences between male and female to impinge on her or him, or to form a life-style.

Thus a woman can go through life without ever being consciously affected very deeply by, say, producing children; she prefers to forget that she ever was a mother. Or, again, a man can go through life not with the usual masculine pre-occupations, but rather as an earnest student of feminine matters.

One way of looking at this which can be fruitful, we suggest, is in the old Hindu saying 'man is the burning-glass that concentrates the woman's multifarious energies'. His masculinity to which his given constitution is likely to afford him direct access is outward-looking, control, abstraction, concentration, extraversion. He is not to the same degree a direct source, as woman is. But man has gone too far; his masculine values have created a tormented world. In the face of the world that man has made, each man must now be a humble student of what is otherwise possible to the woman, through her physical nature, her sex. 'Anatomy is destiny', what outcries are raised about that harmful little slogan! Just as the eye has the destiny of seeing, if it is to be an eye at all, so the bodily organs are openings to ranges of experience. For example, a sexual, as opposed to a gender, difference, appears to be that the woman is capable by nature of multi-orgasm. This means that on the face of it she has a deeper access to the range of experiences we call sexual, than the man has. It is known that gender differences can be unlearned; it is not yet known how far sex differences can be unlearned also. Men can learn multi-orgasm to an extent, but it is nothing like the sexually-experienced woman's multi-orgasms: man's anatomy is just not up to that kind of response on the physical level. It is possible for a man to participate deeply in the menstrual rhythm, so that his whole body responds, even to the sympathetic accumulation of fluid during the pre-menstrual week, and the pattern of dreaming, with some creative resolution arrived at with the period arriving in his female partner; however, he is still experiencing through that partner, and she is the source of this, not him. It is not easy to see how a man could ever use his body to create physically another person, a child; though the scientists do what they can in their intrusive way by making test-tube babies. However, Tantric tradition tells how a man by becoming the sexual and spiritual student of the woman may learn multi-orgasm, may learn to follow the flux and reflux of energies patterned in her fertility cycle, and in partnership with her may learn to produce his own children: but they are spiritual children, ideas, works of art that have the tinge of both partners, discoveries that have the quality of both genders.

Michelene, in the following answers to your questions, we'd like the reader to bear in mind that before we met Peter had been through a Jungian training, which tended to iron out gender differences, and also, as a poet, he has always possessed a strongly feminine side.

Michelene: If gender is important, can you say to what extent you are consciously aware of its importance, i.e. does it come before or after you have written something (and does this apply more to individual or joint writing?) – or is it something that operates at an unconscious level as well? Can you perhaps say which/how – and is there a difference between, say, poetry and non-fiction?

Penelope and Peter: Gender was important in the beginning, but in a somewhat curious way. Penelope happened to be best-known as a novelist, Peter as a poet. When we encountered each other, our desire quite strongly seemed to be to *attempt to become the other*. The mental aspect of this union, which began simultaneously with the physical side, was that Peter began to write novels, and Penelope to write more poetry. There was a kind of circulation of energies. Sex-difference was important, clearly, as Peter has the penis and Penelope the vagina. However, as all lovers who become practised know, it is sometimes difficult to remember who has the penis and who is being penetrated during the excitements of the act.

A variation of the usually-accepted masculine-feminine roles became important during the preliminary dream-work for *The Wise Wound*, our book about menstruation. Penelope dreamed the menstrual dreams, and Peter, by analysing them, reflected them back to her to stimulate the development of the dream-story. Thus, instead of our usual flexible situation, Penelope was the Sybil and Peter her Scribe. However, since that time, in the majority of our work, either of us may be the visionary, and either one of us the critic or analyser; the circulation between us is at the heart of the work, but who takes which role is not important. If there is any emphasis at all, Penelope continues to give Peter improved access to attitudes that result in prose fiction; to an extent Peter performs the reverse role with poetry.

It is of course the analytic or reflecting function which is usually considered to be the masculine role. In this respect, Jung has a good remark on gender roles. He says that the Masculine spirit tends towards perfection, but neglects completeness; the Feminine tends towards completeness, but tends to neglect perfection. By and large, we do not think of each other as that man or that woman; we think of each other as Peter and Penelope; and in writing each is simultaneously the other's Sibyl and Scribe. We are trying to suggest that men and women learn from each other, but, because woman has been feared and betrayed, there is a balance due, and this has to be redressed by work on the man's part.

Michelene: Can you say something more about what point in your writing lives each of you saw your distinct genders impinging on your writing. Was it always? Since feminism? In spite of feminism?

Penelope and Peter: Perhaps we could sum it up by saying that the origin of our work seems to be a conversation between two sides of ourselves, which might as well be called masculine and feminine, as these are the two human opposites. This conversation can be an inward conversation, and this is the tendency in much poetry, we think – between two sides of the one author. But it can be an outward conversation too, as we have indicated just now, in which one's partner takes up the role appropriate for the moment, of Source or Scribe, of Radiation or Focussing-Glass. The 'outer circulation' seems more appropriate in the longer wanderings and conversations of prose fiction or non-fiction, than it does in the shorter pieces which are poetry, the more inward-looking forms. The important point though is that we need these two sides to see with, just as we need two eyes, to get normal stereoscopic three-D vision. So sometimes the interplay is within, and sometimes it is between the two individuals in partnership. Of course the Women's Movement has offered great gifts to human personality, in criticising so radically the lop-sided masculine world. One can only hope it is not too late! Feminism has also begun to address itself to the task of showing how the two sexes can live in complementary partnership, with the male developing his feminine gifts and the female developing her masculine ones.

An important gender difference that has arisen during the past few years is due to Penelope's motherhood. The difference continues long after the actual birth of our daughter Zoe because Penelope as the bearer of the child has (as we say above) a greater or more privileged access to physical communion with that child. Peter could learn this, but it happens that Zoe's own temperament has not directed her relationship with him into that form of male mother. The exigencies and emergencies of socialised gender difference operate here, as Peter has become chief breadwinner, and this directs him into a more conventional father-role than we might otherwise have preferred. Penelope's motherhood affects our work together because when she stops being a mother, and Zoe is in bed or at school, Penelope must then gather herself out of that gender role to become Penelope the dual-gender writer again. Then our partnership can operate as we have described with fluid and flexible gender role-playing, or simple alternation of function. Similarly, Peter must gather himself out of the gender-role he presents while bread-winning, which is still in this world a masculine stereotype, to become Peter again.

Michelene: Can you say whether one or the other of you takes initiative in the writing, or do you take initiative over different things?

Penelope and Peter: Obviously Penelope began *The Wise Wound* by having near-suicidal menstrual distress, but normally we couldn't distinguish the initiative. If scholars should ever be interested in the generation of our work, it would become a small industry for them, since we exchange and use for our individual purposes each other's ideas and images so freely. They will have a well-nigh impossible task untangling which was whose! You remember *The Hermaphrodite Album*, our joint book of poems? The interchange between us was so close with this poetry that we decided not to sign the individual poems with the gender names Peter or Penelope. This seemed to infuriate critics, who wanted to know whether it was a man or a woman who had written a given poem.

Michelene: As poets, do you find some received imagery problematic? Sexual imagery, in particular?

Penelope and Peter: Well, it seems to us that the old saying 'No sex, please; we're British!' is more or less true. People in England appear to know very little about sex and care less. As Beryl Bainbridge remarked in an entertaining review recently of *An English Madam*, by Paul Bailey, about a famous brothel patronised by 'kinky' Members of Parliament and Bishops of the Church, it is remarkably difficult to discover anything about other people's sexuality. Most writers simply don't put it into their books, though we do. Is this what you mean by 'received'? If so, we think that received ideas about sex don't tell a fraction of the whole story. Here the Women's Movement has offered its gifts; we think in particular the feminist insistence on masturbation on its own or as a preparation for high orgasm or loving intercourse, masturbation as a sexual resource known to most women and guiltily practised by most men. Also there is the role of fantasy in good sex, insisted upon by many feminist writers, and here the men can learn a lot; and also feminism will of course insist that if there are active and passive roles in sexuality, they should not be confined to male and female partners exclusively. We may have helped a little in this, in showing in *The Wise Wound* the importance of the intensification and alternation of sexual feelings during the menstrual cycle, that neglected rhythm that men have taught women to see completely negatively. Maybe we have helped redress the balance here, a little.

In another sense of 'received', it is true that Peter gets a lot of his imagery spontaneously during the sort of sex we practise. For example, the whole of his Poetry Book Society Choice, *The Weddings at Nether Powers*, was written in the 'afterglow' of frequent sex during Penelope's pregnancy with Zoe. The deeper or 'uterine' orgasms were very strong indeed while she was carrying, and Zoe in the womb seemed to participate in our love-making. This creative 'afterglow' appears to be a state mediated to Peter by sex predominantly. Penelope seems to have a better natural access to this state by the natural variations in her body. This may be a sex-difference between us, rather than a gender difference, except that Peter can catch the glow from Penelope very easily without necessarily making love. It is possible that in the man, if he is presenting stereotyped gender role-playing as breadwinner, access to the creative state is more difficult for him, and that lovemaking and sex is the most direct bridge to the creative state, and restores the fluidity of personality that is needed then, and unites again thought with feeling, and head with body, for it is clear that the masculine game is played mostly in the head.

Michelene: Do you see your writing as transcending gender? fulfilling gender? confronting gender? circumscribed by gender?

Penelope and Peter: We see writing as one of the most efficient techniques there is of self-examination and of contemplating the world, and for confronting gender, fulfilling it, and transcending it.

Chapter 19

IMAGINATION AND GENDER
Pam Gems

It is difficult to write about being a writer. It's possible to write about being a woman, perhaps a woman writer . . . even a feminist writer. But in the end you're forced to the centre of it, which is about the writing itself – the act and nature of the occurrence. And here, as I say, there are problems.

People constantly ask if, being a woman, you are a feminist. Do you write as a feminist (or as a socialist, or as a 'committed' writer)? And, if you are a wet mix, you try to please with your answer, to placate, even reassure? There is never a question without implied need. To be honest, I tend to find the questions insulting. I don't know why, and I don't know if other writers feel the same, perhaps not, anyway, there is a tendency to lie when you don't know the answers. To make something up. As I say, to reassure. Because the fact is, the sort of writer you are is irrelevant, to the writer. The questions are, one: am I a writer? And two: what is a writer? Is trying to write a way of placating boredom? A way of imposing yourself, getting rich and famous? Is it a retreat into a world that you *can* manipulate, that *does* have order? If that is so, writing is a fascist act . . . I've often suspected it. Or a wank. No doubt it's both, all or none.

To start from another junction. I don't see how you can write other than from yourself. If you're a woman you're bound to write as a woman. There is a question of degree. Certainly in the last twenty years there has been a move from the more neutered, romanticised or intellectualised depiction of women. Even the broad centre of lighter fiction which was traditionally regarded as women's world – that is, senti-mental and soft-gutted stories about love and flowers and romance, cooking and pretty things – have been replaced by raunchy tomes that have been commercially packaged/ computerised and are making fortunes for the publishing houses and perpetrators. Progress? Perhaps. At least now the fact that women menstruate is treated with less fear and superstition. But the commercial exploitations of new freedoms is depressing. Today's chemically mutated woman has been released from the murderous dangers of traditional childbed. We are able to begin to explore, to become aware of ourselves autonomously, to be on our own feet, and to write – and rewrite our own history. We have to discover who and what we are. We must discern our own needs, our demands, in order to know what our contribution should relevantly be. And of course a woman writer cannot but be involved in this vital and exciting and profound movement. Being allowed in, being asked to join is one thing. But we are half the world, and this demands proper accommodation.

These matters intrigue and compel. But writing is another matter. It is individual. When you write you bring the whole of yourself to the meristem, to the growing point of your thought. You are an explorer. You try to push on, to find out. Writing is science, and, like science, not entirely cognitive. In fact often hardly so at all. In other words, whatever your thoughts may be on an issue of the day, however strong your views may be, you are likely, at the point of writing, to find the 'discoveries' coming from the pen or off the typewriter of seeming irrelevance. To find out, when you think you've been writing about social deprivation, that you've been on about your own dodgy marriage can be a let-down. Feeling banal is one of a writer's many curses. But there you are. The pain in Arthur Miller's plays, for example, comes from the personal – the themes are often the husks, the metaphor. All you can do is trust the material and try to make sense of it.

So there is something unbidden about, as the Americans call it, 'Creative Writing'. Something you either deride as psychological hooha, or revere as magic. It depends where you stand. Whether you write, as I say, open-ended, or for a political, social, or commercial purpose. The latter is often disguised as the former, it's known as the bandwagon. You hope, if you're serious, to write out of inadvertence. To surprise yourself, to traduce as little as possible. I have such reverence for writers who are true explorers, who break form and content, who have that generosity which breeds vitality. And a particular fear of writing which finds it necessary to beat the drum, lay down party lines – the fashionable stuff. There's a sort of hatred in the put-down. Which reminds me of the great heresy of our movement, the hatred of men which pervades so much writing, often by implication only, by exclusion; but there. Naturally feminism attracts many women who have been damaged by men, and who can now find areas of real protection and succour. But we're all perfectly well aware of the reverse of it: children, boys as well as girls, driven out of themselves by the age of four by cold mothers. I have sometimes wondered why there hasn't been more backlash, militant groups formed by men, in retaliation. And I honestly believe that it is because many men have moved on, do understand and realise the nature of the oppression of women. There will always be the chauvinists among us, of both sexes, the insecure who need to dominate. But in these times of viciously imposed unemployment, tension between men and women becomes more and more a form of social suicide. We have to stand together. Right, you might say, if you feel so strongly, do a play about it. But it doesn't work that way. What you might feel as a citizen does not always infect or inform the writing. Or if it does, tangentially. You try, you start, and find you've written a musical about three girls who meet at a dance studio and fall in love with one another. I'm not alone in this. I know other writers experience it.

If what I'm trying to say seems frivolous, then that's good. I fear serious writing very much indeed. When I pay for my ticket and go through the door, I want to be engaged, to be filled with life. But I don't want to be told, to be seen off. We're a predatory species. One of the lovely things about having been part of women's groups is the occasional feeling of true camaraderie, of absence of hierarchy. It doesn't always happen, sometimes there's spite, dissension, we're none of us perfect. But there have been such real insights in the last ten years, and some important refusals to go with power structure. I remember a particular incident. We were about to open a play at the Roundhouse, and the two women directors of the piece were sitting in the theatre cafeteria, being interviewed. The rest of us, eating doughnuts at the next table, listened in. The questioner, a young man from a radio station, asked a very long and involved question about the aims and objectives of our group. What did we hope to achieve? Did we want to change society, and if so, how? Were we attempting to introduce a new bias into theatre, create a new sphere of influence? There was a silence, a very long silence indeed. It became embarrassing. At the next table we began to sweat, we needed the free publicity of this interview. Then one of the directors shrugged, pulled a face, and said idly, 'Oh, I don't know.' And it was startling. And totally refreshing to hear a response so open, so unexploitative of the situation. It's become a key phrase – very salutary when you feel a touch of the gnomics coming on. It's so much more relaxing to admit that you don't know. It removes weight, imposition, tension. It opens doors.

Chapter 20

ART AND REASON
Eva Figes

Michelene: When did you start writing?

Eva: I didn't start writing novels until my late twenties, and my first novel was published in the mid-1960s. Then, after the first couple of novels, I wanted to branch out a bit, I was working on my third novel, and I wanted to leave my office job and I also wanted to write social and literary comment and criticism. *Patriarchal Attitudes* was my first non-fiction book – a book about women.

Michelene: How did that come about?

Eva: I hadn't thought about it in advance – I got very angry one day when a woman came round to see me and asked me for things like old clothes for jumble sales for unmarried or separated mothers, and I got very angry, not at her particularly, but at the sort of attitude of charity. I said, you've got to change the laws, you've got to change people's attitudes, and she said, That takes too long. So that started me off, almost instantaneously. I wasn't even conscious myself of how I felt or what I was going to say at all.

I also started writing for the *Guardian* women's page – Mary Stott was editing it then – and I wrote think-pieces. There was something on Equal Pay, I remember, odd social issues, not necessarily just about women. That was in 1967. I finished my third novel in 1968, and while I was writing it I was researching for *PA*, which was published in 1970.

Michelene: Have you always written fiction/non-fiction in tandem?

Eva: Until now, yes. Originally it was stretching another part of my mind that wasn't being used in fiction. Novel-writing is a much more intuitive, exploratory process. It's a division I felt when I was a schoolgirl. I wanted to be a writer then – I thought I was going to be a poet – and even then I was aware that I had other faculties which I thought might get in the way of poetry. Of course, in a sense it doesn't, because you need that critical sense as a novelist as well, but I have on the whole tended to divide up my activity in those two ways. I find that non-fiction writing is a great release because it's so easy for me; once you've done your homework and got your facts right, it's like putting a knife through butter.

Michelene: Do the two kinds of writing give you a different relationship to the real world?

Eva: Yes, and that's one of the reasons why I've written non-fiction. I've usually been motivated by a sense of anger or outrage or impatience with things and I want to make other people see it.

Michelene: So there's a clear political function to your non-fiction?

Eva: Oh yes. Very much so. I was clear when I wrote *PA* that I was writing polemic, I wasn't writing an academic book and it had a function as polemic. I had to batten down the hatches and make sure I didn't leave any loopholes because I was trying to press home an argument in the most effective way.

Michelene: So what is different when you write a novel?

Eva: Well, in the first instance it's a much more intuitive thing. Instead of rationally picking your topic because that's what you think needs doing, with a novel, your topic picks you, it chooses you. You may start with an image or some tiny incident or some vague anecdote and things focus around it; if they don't, then the idea's no good and it stops itself. You're partly discovering things about yourself and your own experience – but I always seem to look ahead and imaginatively solve problems that might be coming up in life. But it's not as specific as that in the early stages; I think you only find out what it's about when you've done it, at the important, the deepest level.

Michelene: Can you see any connections in terms of gender, between the two genres? I mean, in your non-fiction you are very much a woman writing about women at a time when feminism has provided a lot of urgency.

Eva: I think with hindsight that my rational, non-fiction writing has in fact reconditioned me at the intuitive level; I was brought up to accept certain things about my own gender, or at least to take them in and only protest at a very subliminal level, but this process of writing polemical stuff – which after all is an education to oneself as well as to everyone else – has affected the way I write about women in my fiction, and I see that now. For example, in my early novels I tended to concentrate most of my energy into my male characters. After I had written *PA* (though it might have happened anyway, in that your control of the novel changes as you get older) then I started taking female characters much more centrally; things that I was repressing or keeping in the background in order to keep them under control were then able to come out. I suppose it was a question of understanding – that once you understand a problem from every angle then you don't have this danger of things getting out of hand, which can ruin a novel; and I did feel that if I was going to have a woman character she would inevitably become me and that was not on. Though if you take a man as a character, it is an aspect of yourself anyway. In the novel I've just finished I found it was far easier to identify with the male characters, because it's set in 1900 and when you think of the social inhibitions on women at that time, it is actually very hard to put yourself imaginatively into it. But it does depend on many factors.

Michelene: Will you continue writing the two genres in tandem?

Eva: Well, after fifteen years of doing it, I feel I'm getting to the end of it. I suspect I've written my last non-fiction book. I don't really care to give opinions any more; I've given my opinion on the things I feel most strongly about – women and literature – and I feel that fiction is now what's most important. I think that in the non-fiction I was fulfilling a role more as a citizen, and in the novels as an artist. I now feel that I want to function as an artist, and it's time for other people to change the world if they're ever going to. For what it's worth I've done my little bit. My time is running out and so it has become too valuable. I think perhaps that it's also because I'm more confident about the fiction; I'm getting better at it and therefore it takes more out of me; it's therefore more worth while giving everything to it.

Chapter 21

A WOMAN WRITER
Margaret Drabble

I have spent so long pondering the advantages and disadvantages of being a woman writer that on some issues I have thoroughly confused myself. I think I hold the position that as there is nothing wrong with being a woman (a bold enough statement in some ways) so there is nothing wrong with being a woman writer. One should object to being described as a lady novelist, but only on grounds of terminology. There is nothing pejorative about being described as a woman novelist, for women have always been as good at the job as men. I never thought of looking for an insult in the phrase, just as it never occurs to me that it is an insult to be described as an English writer, or a British writer, or even as a writer born in Yorkshire. It is a fact, that's all. And some women novelists are very different from men novelists. Some aren't. As a sexual adjective in this context can only be descriptive, and not discriminative, I don't see why one should object to it, as some do. But I haven't always thought this, and maybe I will change my mind yet again, when some new evidence of real discrimination and prejudice, from a reader or a reviewer, is brought my way. I simply discount people who say they don't read women novelists. They probably don't read men novelists either. Why should they? I don't particularly want everyone to read my books. I wouldn't mind being described as a woman doctor, or a woman pilot, if I were one, so long as it didn't imply that I was bad at the job. And I think women who feel that they object to being called women writers show a certain lack of confidence in their own work. But I may of course be wrong. I've no intention of being dogmatic about the issue.

It is true that in some areas one does meet a positive

hostility towards the woman writer. Some men simply don't like women who do anything at all, out of unthinking traditional prejudice, or out of real fear. Some people, of both sexes, don't like what women have to say these days – Edna O'Brien has said so many unwelcome truths that she has been attacked in the most unreasonable terms by the most reasonable of people, and the issue here is surely sexual. And some men quite genuinely, and with some cause, resent the apparently superior freedom of the woman writer. This issue is bound up with so many others that it can hardly be distinguished, but it's something I'd like to discuss here, because I haven't seen it discussed often before. A few years ago I think I said to some interviewer that I thought some women found it easier to settle down to writing than men because they had husbands to support them, therefore they didn't have to (and in many cases, because of small children, couldn't) work: this was interpreted by another paper, which I think I would have tried to sue if I had read it in time, as my saying that all women novelists including myself lived off their husbands and wrote for amusement. That's not the point for the moment: the point is, is it true that women are at a positive advantage in the career of novelist, because they don't have to earn their livings? To some women, this is clearly an irrelevant issue, but what of those married women who write while their children are small, and succeed in establishing themselves? Would they have had the energy to do it, if they had had to work full time at something else? There have been plenty of writers in the last decade who have started work in precisely this way – one could say that the poor things wrote bitterly out of frustration, loneliness and misery, or one could say that they were lucky to be given the chance and the leisure to feel such productive emotions. (Several men I know, it must be admitted, have been propelled to write by exactly the same emotions – one, doing a very dull job packing exam papers, took a box of paper home in desperation and wrote his first successful work.) Men evidently do resent the feeling that women are leisurely part-time workers, free to dabble in non-remunerative pursuits: Auberon Waugh once reviewed a novel by Nina Bawden by commenting on the fact that it was all very well for lady writers to write when their husbands could support them by good jobs in the BBC. Doctors and lawyers have said to me that if they didn't have a job to do and a family to keep, they too could write. I usually reply by saying that many women have families to keep and do other jobs as well as writing novels, but I rarely quite have the nerve to take the next political step, which is to assert that rearing small children is extremely arduous, and that anyone who has the energy to write novels at the same time is not a dilettante but a miracle of will power and perseverance, employing more energy a day than most men in most jobs I have observed.

There is, however, a real problem here. I met a friend the other day, a writer, who had just returned from a visit to the States, and she said that a pattern was developing there whereby the husband, who had a good well-paid job, would quite often take three days at home with the children, while his wife went off 'to try to be a writer'. I don't know what I feel about this. I ought to approve but I'm not sure if I do. The other thing that worries me slightly is that women seem at times to get positively preferential treatment, once they are established. Getting oneself established may be a sweat, but once a woman has made it – this is true in any sphere – how the press and television will love her, particularly if she is reasonably photogenic and smiles a lot in a suitable feminine manner. Out of a group of mixed writers, it is usually the woman who gets photographed, interviewed, asked to sit on committees. I am not quite sure what one's political response to this ought to be. How should one react to the role of being the statutory woman writer in a gathering? Demand equal representation? Refuse to serve? Graciously accept, as one might an offered seat in a tube, or a hand with one's luggage?

These might seem trivial issues, but they're not really, they are the stuff of daily life. And they do also point to the area in which I think women now may have the most profound and well-earned advantages: the area of subject matter. It is commonplace to deplore the dearth of large or heroic issues in Britain today – how much better to have Vietnam, how much finer to write of South Africa. The British novel will die without its causes. But women have causes still – plenty of them, as the growing interest in Women's Liberation demonstrates. And the novel is the ideal place to voice them, discuss them, try them out. The large amount of fiction written by women in the last decade, since the highly significant publication of Doris Lessing's *Golden Notebook*, bears witness that a lot of women started to worry about the same things at the same time, and turned to fiction to express their anxieties – not only because, traditionally, and despite the spread of education, they still had nowhere else to turn, but also because fiction is ideally suited to such themes. Many of the Women's Liberation proposals cannot be brought about through a change in the law (though some can and should) – they are matter of a shift in public opinion, a change in attitude of women to themselves, of men to women, of women to men. These shifts and changes cover every area of human life, from the most incidental to the most profound: they involve how we behave socially, at parties and after parties, how we spend our money, how we treat our employers and our employees, how we behave sexually and domestically. Many people read novels in order to find patterns or images for a possible future – to know how to behave, what to hope to be like. We do not want to resemble the women of the past, but where is our future? This is precisely the question that many novels written by women are trying to answer: some in comic terms, some in tragic, some in speculative. We live in an unchartered world, as far as manners and morals are concerned, we are having to make up our own morality as we go. Our subject matter is enormous, there are whole new patterns to create. There is no point in sneering at women writers for writing of problems of sexual behaviour, of maternity, of gynaecology – those who feel the need to do it are actively engaged in creating a new pattern, a new blueprint. This area of personal relationships verges constantly on the political: it is not a narrow backwater of introversion, it is the main current which is changing the daily quality of our lives. The truest advantage of being a woman writer now is that never before, perhaps, have women had so much to say, and so great a hope of speaking to some effect.

(*Books on Women*, Spring, 1973; National Book League)

Chapter 22

ME AND MY SHADOWS
Fay Weldon

I once asked an Argentinian psychoanalyst, working in London, whether she found any culturally determined difference between women of various nationalities, and she replied yes, indeed: English women always start by saying 'I'm sorry to take up your time, doctor. I know there are others far worse off than me – it's just that . . .' and then, thus properly prefaced in their own eyes, begin. No other race of women, in her experience, are so determined to underrate their own need, dismiss their own suffering, diminish their own abilities, or, indeed, disclaim their own achievements.

I am, it seems, very English. I preface my own many visits to doctors in just the same way. Asked to write about myself I become apologetic, afraid of boasting, revealing intimacy or claiming an importance to which I am not entitled.

Answering direct questions, however, and thus obliging the interviewer, comes with comparative ease. It seems useful, therefore, to split myself into two (a simple task) and conduct my own interview, courteously, with myself, asking the questions which do usually give some difficulty. Thus:

Interviewer: Do you write regularly or do you wait for inspiration to strike?

Answer: I am glad you asked me that question, since it is the first one usually asked, and I am always uncertain of the reply that is wanted. The one I give, 'I try to do one but end up doing the other', sounds false to my ears, and is clearly unsatisfactory to the questioner. I think the difficulty is that they, asking, and me, replying, are in fact trying to determine the very nature of writing. Is it something that anyone can do, given sufficient intelligence, time, application and discipline? Or is it something more mysterious, some force welling up from (if you like) the group unconscious, which selects a few chosen individuals through which to work? (I used to think the first, but begin to think the second.)

Or perhaps the question merely sounds odd to me, and not to others, because if you write for long enough and often enough, it becomes in the end as natural a function as breathing or eating, and it's like being asked 'Do you eat regular meals or do you wait until you're hungry?' You hardly know what to reply. Perhaps the answer to your question had better be that inspiration only strikes when you have a pen in your hand.

Interviewer: Where do you write?

Answer: I write in any room in the house where no one else happens to be. I often think I write such short paragraphs because I'm interrupted so frequently ... it certainly sharpens the wits.

I have four sons, with over twenty years between the eldest and the youngest. Having a baby gets so much nicer when you're older as you're not thinking of the other things you could be doing. Yet there's a feeling among people that it's wrong to have babies if you're over thirty, rather as youngsters think it's weird for anyone over twenty-five to be having regular sex.

Interviewer: You said earlier that splitting yourself into two was easy. Why did you say that?

Answer: I was comforted recently to read a paperback – *Sybille* – about an American girl with a split personality, call them A and B. A believed herself perfectly normal and ordinary, except she was troubled by having periods of blackout which lasted for hours or weeks and what happened during these blackouts she did not know. Personality B, wilder and more delinquent, knew well enough. During these times, B was in charge of the body. B knew about A and found her boring and trite. A knew nothing about B. After treatment the personality split more and more until there were as many as sixteen different personalities in the same person, some nice, some nasty, some helpful, some destructive, most knowing to one degree or another about the existence of some, but only some, of the others. Eventually, as childhood

traumas were revealed, one personality did develop which
could incorporate them all and Sybille, whole but battered,
retired to run a Ladies' College of Education in some quiet
state.

Interviewer: (interrupting) Comfort, did you say?

Answer: Yes. How else other than in terms of split personality am I to explain the manner in which the circumstances
of my life fit into the nature of the work I happen to be
writing, and that the work precedes the situation: and at the
end of a week in which I cannot remember having written at
all, typescript is neatly stacked waiting for delivery – neatly,
when I am neat in nothing else? Or that when I read for the
first time what I have written it comes to me as something
new?

Interviewer: You mean you detect various divisions in
yourself?

Answer: Yes. A lives a kind of parody of an NW lady
writer's life. Telephones ringing, washing machine over-
flowing, children coming and going, and so on. B does the
writing. B is very stern, male (I think), hard working, puritanical, obsessive and unsmiling. C is depressive, and will sit
for days staring into space, inactive, eating too much bread
and butter, called into action only by the needs of children. A
knows about C but very little about B. B knows about A and C
and in fact controls them, sending them out into the world to
gather information but otherwise despising them. C is
ignorant of A and B – and although A and B leave her notes,
advising her at least to tidy the drawers or sort the files so as
not to waste too much of the lifespan, C has not the heart or
spirit to act on them.

Interviewer: Which one is answering the questions?

Answer: A, of course. Or to answer your question another
way, the writing of fiction, for me, is the splitting of the self
into myriad parts. It's being author, characters, readers,
everyone. B can always focus his mind in spite of A's social
hysteria. All B needs to work, after all, is pencil and paper. A
runs round getting B's work typed, and bringing him cups of
coffee and spending his money.

Interviewer: I am beginning to get the impression that A is
B's wife.

Answer: Are you?

Interviewer: Tell me about your background.

Answer: Well, I was brought up in an all-female environment, and I went to a convent school. I didn't discover men until I went to university. It came as a great shock. It didn't occur to me that men could suffer or have the same aspirations and disappointments that I had. In fact, it took me a very long time to believe that men were actually human beings. I believed the world was female, whereas men have always believed the world is male. It's unusual for women to suffer from my delusion.

I think it gave me a slight advantage over some women. As a writer I'm not conscious of what Virginia Woolf described as 'the angel in the house'. I'm not conscious of someone breathing over my shoulder and whispering: 'Be good. Please men.' As a writer, I can free myself from the need to be liked, appreciated and not disapproved of by men. But in spite of everything, I still find myself being conventionally female. I still want to be an angel – to be supportive, gentle and lovable–and always to be *there*.

Interviewer: Do you mind being called a lady writer?

Answer: Not particularly. I am a writer and I am female. I certainly assume (though I know I am wrong) that my readers are all women. If that is redressing the balance just a little, that's no bad thing. Most men writers – and they are certainly in the majority – assume they are addressing a male audience. And if my women characters are more rounded than the men, this too is redressing a balance so far tilted as to be all but unworkable. I have always written about women because I am a woman, number one, and that is what preoccupies me. Certainly I am criticised for making my male characters nasty but I don't think they are nasty. The point is I just make them behave, talk, and I don't add any justification for their behaviour. Whereas my women characters are all explained.

Interviewer: What about feminism?

Answer: I chose my life-style a long time ago, before the Women's Movement, or women's consciousness was talked about. I was an unmarried mother in the 1950s and that was a salutary experience. I chose a life which seemed to provide good, and it has in many many ways, but I've also encountered the frustrations, the helplessness, the feelings of compromise and desperation which are in my characters. I don't call them autobiographical but I do believe that I am all of them to some degree.

I wasn't aware of all those problems. It only came later. What I've been saying since in the plays and novels encapsulated all the things one should have been saying then but didn't because women's groups didn't exist. I think one has to be forgiven for that, rather as the Roman Catholics will forgive you for not being a Christian if you were born in a time before Jesus.

In the end I saw that what I was writing about could actually be organized into an ideology, a movement. Eventually it becomes clear that your interests and other people's current preoccupations coincide.

Interviewer: What about other women writers?

Answer: Writers of my own generation tend to be established by now and aren't actually dealing with the things which I tend to wish to deal in. And the young ones, by and large, tend to be much more didactic. I mean they're much more *consciously* didactic.

I grew up not knowing what was happening to women and why, and now everyone knows that is happening. But knowing that makes younger women's writing more conscious than mine was.

And yet, you see, the sources of my indignation are for me the same as they are for other women in the Women's Movement who are better fitted to analyse and to see how things can be changed.

I want to lead people to consider and explore ideas that aren't very popular, which many people would rather not think about. But if anybody's to get anywhere, they had better think about it. One *can* transcend one's body: whether it's good to do so is another matter.

Interviewer: Do you prefer in reviews to be called Miss, Ms or Mrs?

Answer: B, being male, finds all titles quite irrelevant. A finds Miss irritating, since it is inaccurate, and awarded as a courtesy of the most insulting kind, but is, unfortunately, mostly found in approving reviews. Ms, unless used ironically and unpleasantly (as it frequently is) indicates at least some kind of awareness in the reviewer. Mrs (also used sometimes as an insult) appears mostly in bad reviews. You may draw what conclusions you wish from this as to the status of the woman writer in our society today. Fay! I would prefer to have a neutral name, like Saturday or Colonnade, but that is scarcely possible.

Interviewer: Do you consider yourself a fortunate person?
Answer: Yes.
Interviewer: I don't think we have time for any more.
Answer: No.

Based on interviews in: *Guardian*, 20 September 1976;
Evening News, 12 February 1980; *Observer Magazine*,
18 February 1979; *Gay News* no. 185.

NOTES ON CONTRIBUTORS

Most of the writers spread their writing interests and skills over different genres, so the following information is merely to provide an indication of what they are best known for, or write most of:

Nora Bartlett: novels and criticism.
Sara Maitland: novels, short stories and Christianity.
Judith Kazantzis: poetry, criticism.
Wendy Mulford: poetry.
Libby Houston: poetry.
Cora Kaplan: literary history and criticism.
Michele Roberts: poetry and novels.
Angela Carter: novels, criticism.
Noel Greig: plays.
Rozsika Parker: art criticism, art history.
Alison Hennegan: journalism.
Andrew Lumsden: journalism.
Jill Tweedie: journalism.
Angela Phillips: journalism.
Mary Stott: journalism, social history.
Irving Weinman: poetry.
Penelope Shuttle, Peter Redgrove: poetry, novels.
Pam Gems: plays.
Eva Figes: novels, social history.
Margaret Drabble: novels, criticism.
Fay Weldon: novels, plays.